GRIT, NOT GLAMOUR

GRIT, NOT GLAMOUR

Female Farmers, Ranchers, Ropers, and
Herders of the American West

CHERYL MULLENBACH

TWODOT®
Essex, Connecticut
Helena, Montana

For Richard L. Wohlgamuth

A · TWODOT® · BOOK
An imprint and registered trademark of The Rowman & Littlefield Publishing Group, Inc.
4501 Forbes Boulevard, Suite 200
Lanham, Maryland 20706
www.rowman.com

Distributed by NATIONAL BOOK NETWORK

British Library Cataloguing in Publication Information Available

Library of Congress Cataloging-in-Publication Data Available

ISBN 9781493060498 (pbk) | ISBN 9781493060504 (electronic)

CONTENTS

Acknowledgments

Thanks to all the dedicated individuals who work at libraries and museums across the country. Their help in locating primary sources, archival photos, and other treasures was invaluable. Special thanks to Alfred McMichael, who offered a unique perspective that only a family member could on the stories of Laura Wallace. Thank you to Kathy Plank for transcription help. RaeAnn Swanson-Evans's professionalism, curiosity, and thoroughness enriched the research experience for me.

INTRODUCTION

"I have been a farmer's wife for thirteen years, and everybody knows that the farmer's wife must of a necessity be a very practical woman, if she would be a successful one. I am not a practical woman and consequently have been accounted a failure by practical friends and especially by my husband, who is wholly practical."[1]

IN 1906, SOMEONE CAME UP WITH AN IDEA TO PRODUCE A BOOK ABOUT ordinary people in the format of firsthand accounts describing their day-to-day experiences. *The Life Stories of Undistinguished Americans as Told by Themselves* features a multicultural array, including "The Life Story of an Itinerant Minister," "The Life Story of a Negro Peon," "The Life Story of an Irish Cook," and "The Life Story of a French Dressmaker." Chapter 9, "The Life Story of a Farmer's Wife," was written by an anonymous—and, by her own admission, not practical—woman who described her days and years as a reluctant farmer and who dreamed of a literary life rich with reading and most importantly writing.

This unnamed and long-forgotten farm woman's voice introduces each chapter of *Grit, Not Glamour*. Her words knit together the stories of a diverse group of individuals who found themselves engaged in farm- and ranch-related enterprises. These intriguing homesteaders, ranchers, growers, livestock dealers, activists, writers, bronco busters, and a couple swindlers are at the core of *Grit, Not Glamour*. Practicality often played a role in their successes and failures, as did desperation, stubbornness, curiosity, humor, bravery, a search for adventure, cravings for learning, hankerings for ways to express their creative sides, and love. In recognizing this collection of individuals, we celebrate the memory of women who devoted their lives to farm- and ranch-related pursuits. Some embraced their roles, others did not, but most would agree their contributions were frequently minimized or overlooked.

Women branding livestock. *The Denver Public Library, Western History Collection, [Z-338].*

Men and women who have lived and worked on a family farm or ranch may relate to the emotions and exploits experienced by the women who are profiled. Town dwellers and urbanites generations removed from the farm or their rural communities, who grew up hearing grandparents' and great-grandparents' stories about life on a ranch or farm, will appreciate these women, who may or may not resemble in any way their foremothers. City slickers who never spent a day on a farm nor thought the life of a rancher was in any way appealing will meet a community of spunky, brazen, plucky (and, in a couple cases, dishonest), hardworking gals who donned trousers, tucked long hair under straw hats, nurtured plants and baby livestock, studied the markets, fretted over the weather, disseminated vital information, scraped animal dung from their boots, and enjoyed a few hours of deep sleep afforded by hours in the fresh country air, only to rise early the next day and start all over again.

Part I

Big Operations

"I was an apt student at school and before I was eighteen I had earned a teacher's certificate of the second grade and would gladly have remained in school a few more years, but I had, unwittingly, agreed to marry the man who is now my husband, and though I begged to be released, his will was so much stronger that I was unable to free myself without wounding a loving heart, and could not find it in my nature to do so. . . . [M]y husband thought it a willful waste of time to read anything and that it showed a lack of love for him if I would rather read than to talk to him when I had a few moments of leisure. . . . I would only read when he was not at the house, thereby greatly curtailing my already too limited reading hours."[1]

Laura Owen Wallace

"A Woman of Fortitude and Indomitable Willpower"

"You have always been my ideal, don't you know?" Laura Deloach Owen Wallace bent to kiss her husband, Daniel Webster Wallace, as he passed "across the Divide to a new frontier where cowboys do not return." It was Tuesday, March 28, 1939, a few days before the couple's fifty-first wedding anniversary, the first Laura would face without her beloved partner, a man widely known as 80 John, "one of the most respected Negro ranchmen in the Old West." Together more than a half century, the pair had conquered extraordinary challenges to build a prosperous business in a land they had first seen "unsullied by barbed wire and train smoke, a cowman's paradise of running water, grass-covered hills and wide fertile valleys."[1]

When Laura Owen met Daniel Webster Wallace in the 1880s in Navarro County, Texas, he was well on his way to an extraordinary life, rich with admirable undertakings and impressive accomplishments. Daniel was born to enslaved parents, William and Mary Barber Wallace, in 1860—shortly after Mary had been purchased for $1,000 and separated from her husband, William Wallace. As a teen, he set out from Victoria County to pursue the life of a cowboy. Driving cattle, taming wild horses, roping, wrangling, and branding—all became part of the young Daniel Webster's day-to-day duties as a hand with some of Texas's early cattlemen. In 1877, he went to work for Clay Mann and stayed with him for fourteen years. As an employee of Mann, he learned all there was to know about ranching and picked up his nickname 80 John. The Mann brand

John Wallace. *Courtesy of the Laura and John Wallace family.*

Laura Wallace. *Courtesy of the Laura and John Wallace family.*

was the number *80* and Daniel Webster seared plenty of *80*s into the backs of Mann cattle. It's unclear how he came by the name John, but for the rest of his life, Daniel Webster Wallace was respectfully known as 80 John.

80 John had invaluable experiences during his stint with the Mann enterprise. "[R]iding in the dust" of Clay Mann's cattle herds, he "saw the last of the buffaloes"; "trailed Comanches who stole his saddle horse"; and "rode up the cattle trails to Abilene and Dodge, Kansas," living his dream in "this cattleman's paradise."[2] He rode Mann's vast holdings in Texas and the lands that became the state of New Mexico, proving his skills as a rider and roper and reliable driver and even spending time in Mexico on one of Mann's ranches. As a typical cowboy, 80 John survived stampedes, outlaws, prairie fires, and treacherous river crossings while managing to avoid the pitfalls found at the ends of the trails in gambling houses and dance halls.

The creed many young cowboys lived by was "It was drink and be merry, spend money and get more."[3] But not 80 John. And Clay Mann noticed this about his trusted cowhand, who always replied, "I will do my best," when asked to complete a job.[4] It was the reason the two men entered into an agreement to help 80 John acquire his first herd. Over a two-year period, Mann paid 80 John only a portion of his wages ($120) and set aside a much larger portion ($600) until the young cowboy had enough money to purchase a herd of steers, which he ran on the Mann range. However, 80 John's cattle had one distinct difference from the other cattle on the range. They were branded with the letters *WALLASE* (later changed to *WALLACE*).[5] And by 1885, 80 John was the proud owner of a piece of land in Mitchell County, Texas.

About this time, 80 John was thinking that he could benefit from a little more formal education beyond the few months he had endured as a youth during breaks from his work in the fields. So for two winters, he set aside his unpleasant memories of switches and dunce caps from his early education—the result of too much daydreaming about becoming a cowboy and sullenness over having to haul wood for the schoolhouse stove—and spent four months attending a school for Black kids in Navarro County, and it turned into a life-altering decision. He purchased twelve acres of land while there, but that was not the most momentous milestone from 80 John's time in the county.

Few details of the courtship of Laura and 80 John have survived. The two met when he spent those months attending school and Laura was finishing her high school education. At more than six feet in stature, he would have been someone who stood out in an elementary classroom, where he was brushing up on the basics. Laura was planning to pursue a career as a teacher, but somehow, 80 John convinced her to join him and embark on a life as a rancher. At the end of his second winter at school, Laura and 80 John went to the Navarro County courthouse in Corsicana and acquired a marriage license from the clerk of court, Baldwin Harle Woods, on April 7, 1888. It was valid for sixty days—plenty of time for anyone to reconsider a decision to go forward with a marriage. But the two didn't need sixty days to know they wanted to spend the rest of their lives together. Twenty-four hours later, the couple returned to the courthouse with a completed form indicating they had been united in marriage—April 8, 1888.

Laura and 80 John lived in a two-room house on one of Clay Mann's ranches when they were first married, and 80 John continued to work for

Mann. After a couple years, the Wallaces decided it was time to become full-time ranchers themselves in Mitchell County near the town of Loraine. They continued to increase their cattle herd and purchase land. John cut posts from native trees to fence their holdings. When they had the money 80 John had earned working for other ranchers at roundups or loading cattle from shipping stock pens, they reinvested it into their ranch or saved for future opportunities. Although they were careful with their earnings in their early years of ranching, 80 John presented his wife with a thoughtful gift after the sale of some steers in the early 1890s. Laura hadn't been back to Navarro County since her marriage in 1888. The sixty-dollar profit from the sale paid for Laura's visit back to see friends and family.

When her husband was gone for periods tending the cattle and maintaining their lands, Laura's loneliness was eased by the bond she made with a large collie dog who had come to live with the Wallaces the first week of their marriage. Tige—because he could be as fierce as a tiger— was devoted to Laura. Sleeping in her bedroom at night and guarding the entry of the house in the daytime, Tige ventured out to rid the yard of snakes occasionally. For those humans who dared to approach Laura, they'd better introduce themselves to Tige before getting too close to her. And that included 80 John if he had been absent for a length of time.

Despite Tige's protective tendencies, the Wallace home became widely known for the owners' "hospitality and spirit of the West." 80 John and Laura welcomed travelers with nourishment and a place to stay for the night. And if the couple was gone for a few days, no problem. Everyone knew the "doors of Wallace's house in those days were never locked."[6] Travelers were welcome to stop in, have a meal, and leave a note.

Shortage of water was a constant challenge for the Wallaces. In the early days of their ranching, only a few scattered wells dotted the landscape. Drilling for water was an expensive endeavor—as much as $2,500.[7] The Wallaces, like many ranchers in the area, bought water from individuals who hauled the precious commodity in huge tanks to the ranches, where the ranchers stored it in barrels. But 80 John seemed to have a knack for locating underground water, and in time, numerous windmills pumping water from wells were scattered across the Wallaces' property.

Laura with grandchildren Vonceil, TP, and Elaine in front of her homestead in 1923 or 1924. The house has been restored and is on display at Texas Tech University in Lubbock, Texas. *Courtesy of the Laura and John Wallace family.*

As the Wallaces' land holdings expanded, they placed some acres in fields for growing crops and entered agreements with tenant farmers. The Wallaces were known for their respectful and fair treatment of tenants. At the beginning of the growing season, 80 John asked the tenants to provide him with an estimate of their expenses for the year. Whatever the amount, the Wallaces generously increased it by a third. The tenants benefited from the arrangement, as did the Wallaces, who realized extra income. The tenants also made Laura's work lighter as she stayed on the ranch, at times alone with children and grandchildren, while 80 John was wintering their cattle on far-off leased pastures or driving cattle to shipping sites.

As their cattle herds grew, both 80 John and Laura worked hard to succeed. Laura had a special connection to the animals. Cold winters meant hardships for the stock. When 80 John came across cows that were suffering from the elements, he brought them home to Laura. Some were too weak to stand. Together they lifted the animals into the special pen they called the "hospital," where Laura did all she could to nurse them back to health.[8] The four-legged patients became known as the "Lady's

Friends."[9] When she couldn't save the weak cows, their hides were dried and sold, and the money was used to buy feed for the surviving herd.

Maud and Pan, the ranch horses used to pull heavy freight wagons to town, taught Laura a lesson the first time she tried to harness the pair and place them in position for a trip to town, her wagon filled with cotton-seed cake and meal from the Wallaces' cotton crop. The team had always appeared to be mild-mannered, but as Laura struggled to place Maud to the right of the wagon tongue, she balked and moved to the left. After more than a few attempts, Laura understood Maud was insisting on her usual position to the *left* of the tongue. Laura didn't make the same mistake twice. And Laura learned early in her ranching days to rely on her faithful team during dangerous trips to town when fifty-mile-per-hour winds drove dust into her face and cut visibility to less than a quarter mile. Even in the dark on the return trip, Maud and Pan never failed to deliver Laura safely to the Wallace spread.

Laura also learned a lesson from the old cows on the ranch who, despite their advanced ages, became quite demanding when it came to nourishment. At the sound of her wagon, brimming with cottonseed cake, apples, and potatoes, the cows always eagerly greeted Laura in anticipation of their tasty meal. One night, as Laura delivered the treats, the cows quickly devoured their usual fare and then aggressively began to chew on her pocketbook!

Laura and 80 John also combined their talents when it came to the business side of their ranching enterprise. When legal agreements and contracts were required, they hired lawyers to draw up the specifics. Before signing, Laura carefully read aloud the documents while her husband committed to memory all the complex details. The Wallaces' devotion to one another endured as they grew old together, and it was often observed by family members. Most nights, 80 John stretched out on his bed after a day in a saddle, and Laura sat nearby with a stack of newspapers and magazines, reading aloud to the man she so admired. "They had a beautiful life together," a granddaughter who spent summers with them recalled.[10] In 1938, an Abilene newspaper carried an article marking the couple's fiftieth wedding anniversary—"Golden Wedding Celebration for Midland Negroes."[11] It presented an overview of 80 John's life and his remarkable journey from cowboy to cattleman and rancher. And although the purpose of the article was to recognize the couple's notable fifty-year relationship, the reporter ignored Laura's contributions to the family enterprise—failing even to include her name!

But family members appreciated the role Laura played in the family. Laura and her husband were a team in their business as well as their personal relationship, and their unique personalities complemented one another. "I know my grandmother had much more influence over his decisions than any of us ever knew," a granddaughter said in a 1995 interview.[12] And when the Wallaces suffered disappointments or setbacks, Laura was an "emotional touchstone," a steady, calming force for her husband.[13]

When 80 John died in 1939, Laura continued to manage the ranch in Mitchell County until her death in 1950 at the age of 80. Not long before her death, Laura had granted an interview to a local newspaper in which

Laura and grandchildren Vonceil and TP in 1919 or 1920. *Courtesy of the Laura and John Wallace family.*

Four generations of the Wallace family in 1950: Laura, daughter Mary, granddaughter Elaine, great-grandson Alfred. *Courtesy of the Laura and John Wallace family.*

she reminisced about her life with 80 John and their early days of ranching with their four children, Mary, Hettye, Eula, and Carson. She talked about old-time acquaintances, the first grocery store and train station in the area, camping in a hut while tending their cattle, and their struggles and triumphs. The reporter wrote about Laura's strong religious beliefs, her enjoyment of the radio, and her delight in petting the white-faced calves on her ranch. She alluded to a touch of rheumatism. Laura didn't bring up her long-ago dream of becoming a teacher; however, she may have been thinking of it when she mentioned that teaching "runs in the family," as she identified several descendants who were educators.[14] A few months after the interview, Laura died in Johnson Hospital in Loraine, Texas. Hettye wrote about her mother, "She was a woman of fortitude and indomitable willpower which gave her courage to live in the West during frontier days."[15]

Laura and 80 John were honored for their business acumen and contributions to ranching history by friends and community members as well as business acquaintances during their lifetimes and after their deaths. Frequently, 80 John was the focus, but family members knew it was nearly impossible to speak of one without including the other. "My father and mother in their married life were always pushing through new frontiers in their sharing of life," Hettye wrote in 1960.[16] And the legacy that Laura and 80 John's descendants chose to inscribe on the couple's shared headstone on the Wallace ranch reads, "With characters of granite, they had hearts of kindness always ready and willing to respond to the call for help."[17]

Frances Pearle Mitchell

Pigs Are a Girl's Best Friend

"PLEASE DON'T MAKE ME OUT A 'PORK QUEEN' . . . WITH HUNDREDS OF little squealing pigs scampering after me," Frances Pearle Mitchell admonished a newspaper reporter writing a feature story in January 1913 about Frances, who managed "her own farm without the advice of a man."

Although Frances *did* raise pigs because "they are so interesting, and noisy and fat, and so shrilly grateful for a bit of chopped corn," she did much more on her three-hundred-plus-acre farm in Boone County, Missouri, about ten miles outside Columbia. When her parents died, Frances took over the family enterprise her pioneering grandparents had built long before she was born. By the time she was five years old, she crawled up the necks of the farm horses to perch on their broad backs, and by school age, she'd devised ways to skip classes at her country school so she could walk behind her dad as he maneuvered the workhorses behind the plow. She started at an early age to offer farming advice to her dad, and he seldom discounted it. She recalled her first experience as a negotiator, when in the absence of her dad, she demanded a price fifty cents per head higher than her father expected for some sheep. "The man had to pay the extra price too, but not until after long, hard wrangling over the price," she said.[1]

Frances eventually completed country school and went on to graduate from Stephens Female College in 1880. Despite missing school as a child to experience the practical side of farming, she came to recognize the value of education as she managed her farm, which she called Forest

Home, "one of the state's most modern farms."[2] She consulted with experts at the University of Missouri in Columbia to keep abreast of scientific advances in agriculture and farm markets. A "well-managed farm" gave women "independence, scientific knowledge, contact with widely different people," Frances said. "And it is my sincere belief that farming is the best profession a woman can follow."[3]

MISS FRANCES PEARLE MITCHELL

Frances Pearle Mitchell. Los Angeles Express, *March 16, 1914.*

A typical day for Frances began about 6:00 a.m., when she performed a few housekeeping duties and then made the rounds inspecting her crops and livestock while directing the work of her employees. She personally hired all her workers and played a big hand in supervising them. At planting time, she chose the best ground for corn or hay or wheat; she marked the places for new fence posts and oversaw the digging and setting of the posts. And while most of the physical labor was performed by her farmhands, Frances could "stretch barb wire as well as cook," according to a local newspaper.[4] She had high standards, and when some haystacks were not made to her liking, she demanded they be redone—showing the workers her methods to ensure proper water drainage. She followed best farming practices: "I raise corn, wheat and hay, rotating my crops according to the demands of the soil." She offered an example of her rotation practices: "This year I am experimenting with corn on land half of which was for two years in red clover and the other six months in stock peas."[5]

Frances loved to travel and divided her time between managing Forest Home and globetrotting to wherever "her fancy takes her."[6] During her absences, she relied heavily on her employees and sometimes her tenants to carry on, guided by very specific written instructions she prepared before leaving. She expected them to be followed precisely.

"Traveling is my passion, but the price of pigs and corn determine whether I run over to Europe or Egypt, or just take a bit of a journey to the Pacific coast or down into Mexico," she said.[7] "Last year while nine months in the Orient and in Europe I had on my farm only hay and corn, which I rented on shares. I sold all corn and stock that were ready, closed the year's business, departed in January and returned in September to attend to the corn gathering, fattening of hogs and selling of calves."[8] Everywhere she visited, she gleaned valuable nuggets of agricultural methods from the local farmers. Some of those ideas she brought back to Missouri to incorporate into her farm operation.

It was in January 1911 that a handful of "practical women farmers" gathered to form the Missouri Women Farmers' Club, a statewide group that chose Frances as their president.[9] They proudly stated the purpose of the group: to celebrate the value of women who managed their own farms. Alice Kinney raised registered hogs on her four hundred acres, Mabel Miller exhibited her Berkshire hogs at county fairs and at state livestock events, and Cora F. Shewell was proud of her dairy cows and the fruit she sold at markets. Maude Griffith Wood, the owner of 1,600 acres of land, much of which was seeded in English bluegrass, was secretary of the club. However, a few years after the formation of the club, Maude made the fatal mistake of turning over the management of her farm to her husband—a strict violation of the club's membership requirements, which stated that membership "depended entirely upon a woman's managing her own farm."[10]

The women were sorry to see Maude go; however, they voiced their concerns that by her actions she had transitioned from a "woman farmer and a charter member" to a "mere farm woman."[11] The group continued to grow, and on their first anniversary, they announced their sponsorship of a permanent scholarship for young women at the College of Agriculture at the University of Missouri, providing the opportunity for a female student to "wrest a living from the broad bosom of mother earth."[12] Frances declared that the club was the "beginning of history in which the woman farmer will figure as the heroine."[13]

Road building and maintenance issues had always been a topic of controversy and debate in the United States. What portion of the cost, if any, should the federal government contribute? What about state, county, or local governments? If the government failed to help, should individual landowners foot the bill for maintenance of the country's roadways? In Missouri, roads were as important to the economic and social welfare of the citizens as they were in the other states. So when Missouri governor Elliot Major looked for a suitable individual to represent the state at the Fourth American Road Congress in Atlanta, Georgia, in 1914, he turned to Frances. Sponsored by the American Highway Association and the American Automobile Association, the six-day event pulled together policy makers, economists, transportation experts, civil engineers, road builders, and others to advocate for better roads in urban and rural parts of the country. While "preaching the gospel of good roads and studying the economics of road building," speakers at the congress covered a wide variety of topics.[14] Virginia's highway commissioner presented an overview of the state's use of convicts (75 percent of whom were Black) for road construction, and New Hampshire's superintendent of highways spoke about the best surfaces for light-volume, mixed-traffic roads (motor propelled and horse drawn).[15] Women attended the congress also but met in a separate location and were offered different presentations. The Women's Conference on Roads featured all female speakers, including Frances, whose introduction must have turned heads: "She has 'bossed road gangs' and superintended the work on the roads near her farm."[16]

She spoke about the building of roads across Missouri over the old Santa Fe Trail, "one of the early commercial trails to the West," and the role women played in pushing for good roads in the state.[17] She spoke about the work of the Missouri Women Farmers' Club, who realized the importance of good roads to reach markets and keep in touch with community interests. Women had organized bands of Boy Road Scouts, who dragged roads and cut weeds along the roadways. Frances talked about a Missouri woman who held a road-dragging demonstration around her farm, encouraging her neighbors to follow suit in maintaining the roads near their farms. A one-room-school teacher organized boys and girls into "squads of road Scouts."[18] In closing, Frances said, "Women can do much by their enthusiasm toward getting the right kind of road legislations and by their demand for the wise and honest expenditure of road funds in their respective States and counties."[19]

In 1914, Frances wintered in California and spoke to a Los Angeles women's club at the Blanchard Music Hall. "Southern California is an ideal place for farming. . . . With its possibilities for close contact with the rest of the world, its climate and other remarkable advantages it should be the easiest and most attractive place on earth to farm," Frances told the audience. The *Los Angeles Express* proclaimed she was in town to "preach the back-to-the-land gospel" and that she was a true believer in the idea. They continued, "With pardonable pride Miss Mitchell admitted that she can stretch a barb wire fence with as much ease and precision as any man in her employ and plow as straight a furrow. She knows how to reap a grain field and build a haystack after the most improved fashion." According to the newspaper, Frances "charmed her Southern California sisters" with her stirring words.[20]

All her life, Frances advocated for women's leadership in the field of agriculture. "A woman can farm successfully if she will stick to the work, have energy, clear judgment and intelligence," she said.[21] And although at one time she tried to distance herself from the pork-queen label, she also recognized the value of the little porkers: "I believe in corn and hogs. A beautiful ring I have, the diamonds of which were bought with the price of one hog, is fairly good proof, I believe, of the value of a pen of pigs."[22]

PART II

A SISTERHOOD

"When critical housewives spend the day with me I always feel that my surroundings appear to a disadvantage. They cannot possibly know the inside workings of our home, and knowing myself to be capable of the proper management of a home if I had the chance of others, I feel like I am receiving a mental criticism from them which is unmerited, and when these smart neighbors tell me proudly how many young chicks they have, and how many eggs and old hens they have sold during the year, I am made to feel that they are crowing over their shrewdness, which they regard as lacking in me, because they will persist in measuring my opportunities by their own."[1]

3

The Lahm Sisters

Minding Their Own Business in Their Own Way

"THE CITY FATHERS OF WILLITS, MENDOCINO COUNTY, ARE CONSIDER-
ing the grave question whether the Lahm sisters shall be permitted
to appear on their streets in masculine garb," the *San Francisco Examiner* reported. "[S]uch is the tremendous question that flutters the City
Fathers."[1]

Gussie and Louise Lahm were most likely too busy holding their
own, "fighting forest fires, recovering stolen cattle and resisting poach-
ers," to allow newspaper headlines to dictate the clothes they put on each
morning in the winter of 1900.[2] Their sheep and cattle ranch, perched
in an almost inaccessible spot high in the mountains of northern California, consumed the young women's days and nights. Blue-jean overalls tucked into their heavy work boots and braided hair piled beneath
leather-trimmed sombreros, the two sisters set out each day determined
to provide a secure life for their little family, consisting of an aging mother
and several cherished canines.

Gussie, nineteen, and Louise, twenty, had spent their younger years
at a convent school in San Francisco, where they acquired some valuable
book learning and debatably useful needlework skills. But their futures
were sidelined one Christmas holiday, when they endured a multiday
blizzard that nearly did their dad in as he tended sheep back home at the
family ranch. As the Lahms watched the snow fall that December day in
the late 1890s, Gussie and Louise's dad, Jacob, a German immigrant and
head of the all-female household, donned his warmest clothing and set

out to round up seven hundred sheep trapped in a gulch behind a steep mountainside, where they would surely die if not attended to.

"I am going to help get those sheep," Gussie later recalled telling her dad. "And I just made father let me."[3]

Working throughout the night in the deepening snow, Gussie and Jacob prodded the chilled sheep to keep moving "till they got some life into them."[4] Returning to the ranch house when daylight broke, the two warmed up in front of a toasty fire and enjoyed a steaming cup of coffee prepared by Louise and Gussie's mother, Louisa.

"Such a sight as I was!" Gussie said, referring to the traditional feminine clothing she had worn throughout the ordeal. "Every time I jumped off that horse I caught my skirt, and it was torn from top to bottom."[5]

It was a turning point for Gussie. The next morning, when she woke to another day of "at least 30 miles of hard riding," she reconsidered those cumbersome skirts, eyed her dad's practical shirt and pants, and made a life-changing decision.[6]

"I put on his clothes and went and I have been doing it ever since," she said.[7]

Jacob was an elderly sixty at the time, and the rugged life of a California rancher eventually took a toll on the old fellow. When he died, the locals thought it was the end of the Lahm ranching enterprise. There were no Lahm sons to take on the physical demands and the complex business challenges of ranching. But those doomsayers underestimated the gritty, no-nonsense Lahm sisters, who regarded ranching "easier than housework" and never looked back to their days of book learning, skirt wearing, and needleworking.[8] By the time Helen Grey-Page, a woman's page reporter for the *Butte Miner*, spent a couple days at the Lahm ranch shadowing the two women for a feature story in February 1900, they had already proved their worth to all but those Willits city fathers who were intent on questioning their clothing.

Three years before, in October 1897, the *San Francisco Call* had run a half-page spread featuring the Lahm sisters. Reporter Lillian Ferguson had written about their "gentle, ladylike demeanor" and their home "perched on a Mendocino crag," where the "flesh and blood heroines" confronted bears, panthers, and coyotes and yet were in no way "coarsened" individuals. Claiming Louise and Gussie were as comfortable in a saddle, trapping game, or branding cattle as most girls were in a debutante drawing room, Lillian declared they were entirely capable of shearing sheep, pitching hay, and lassoing wild steers. Her account of Gussie killing a marauding panther gripped the *Call*'s readers. The beast measured eight feet (eleven feet according to an alternate version of the encounter), weighed two hundred pounds, and had dined too many times on the Lahms' sheep. Gussie secured her prey after tracking him to a canyon and shooting him with her rifle. She then employed a system learned from Jacob—bracing large tree limbs against the horse's side to create a crude ramp which allowed her to maneuver the huge cat carcass onto the horse's back. Lillian wrote about the Lahms' extraordinary relationship with their highly intelligent and exceptionally valuable ($200 apiece, according to the reporter) sheepdogs. These canine "protectors of the flock" proved their worth frequently but especially when wild animals stole lambs. The sisters and their dogs tracked and hunted "to the death" any bear brazen enough to wander into the herd.[9] According to the *Call* reporter, nearly every man, woman, and child in Mendocino County had nothing but respect for the Lahm sisters. But three years later, when city officials in Willits got in a snit about the Lahms' clothing, the *San Francisco Examiner* speculated that plain old green-eyed jealousy sparked the criticism of the highly successful ranch women. Not so, according to certain Willits citizens, who insisted the odd sisters were a spectacle and a source of ridicule from out-of-town visitors, who jeered at the peculiar habits of the young women.

One thing was certain: The sisters were cause for curiosity and not just in California. In April 1900, two national publications, the *Cosmopolitan* and the *Wide World Magazine*, reproduced a lengthy feature story about the girl ranchers of California. The reporter included several photos of the sisters, mostly in their masculine clothing, with at least one dog tucked into each picture.

So when Helen Grey-Page of the *Butte Miner* set out to write a feature story about them, she may have already heard tales about the

GUSSIE LAHM
AND HER DOGS.

Gussie Lahm and her dogs. *University of British Columbia, Wallace B. Chung and Madeline H. Chung Collection, "The Girl Ranchers of California," by W. F. Wade.*

eccentric Lahm sisters. Still, she must have been beyond excited to tackle the assignment that would allow her to spend a few days riding the range with the female ranchers—a welcome distraction from her usual reporting on appropriate skirts for golfing (black duck with ruffles and shirtwaists of sheerest lawn) or proper bonnets for grieving widows (pointed at the front with white crepe ruching). Helen was in for a treat.

Her first day at the ranch was jam-packed with adventure. Not yet out of the home paddock, the lady ranchers stopped to milk a cow that was resisting the hired man's cold hands; negotiated with a passing drover on a fair price for ten cattle; and lassoed, threw down, and branded a critter with a big *L*.

Finally, they were ready to head for the range, hefty bags of salt for the sheep balanced over the horses' backs and rifles handy in anticipation of outlaws, rattlesnakes, or wayward hunters. And although there were surefire laws in place that outlawed trespassing, brash hunters, most of whom "can't tell a quail from a sheep or a cow from a deer," according to Gussie, were constant nuisances for the Lahm sisters.[10]

There was the time Gussie came upon a hot campfire left by a hunter who had boldly trespassed on the Lahm property. Flames were already licking at the trees and brush over a wide swath of scrub as Gussie battled to minimize the damage. As the fire crept toward the Lahms' fence, she desperately fought to save the valuable fencing material.

"Do you see these little white scars all over my hands?" she asked as she recounted the harrowing experience to Helen. "The fence is put together with wire instead of nails; and while tearing down the fence, wires would stick in my hands; and they were red hot."[11]

Fortunately, Gussie had invited the family dog, Perro, to ride with her that morning, and the loyal pooch was eager to help his mistress, who was under obvious duress. As Gussie carefully singed her handkerchief in the hot flames and tied it to Perro's collar, the dog waited for directions. Gussie's command to go home and return with Louise was all he needed to jumpstart his crucial mission. Off he went with the handkerchief message secured around his neck, racing to the ranch to alert Louise of her sister's distress.

Louise and a neighbor, led by Perro, made their way to Gussie, and together they fought the fire all that night and the next day with help from some passersby. Covered in soot and fatigued from the heroic effort, Gussie finally took a break to eat some of the food the men offered. "It was the first time I had sat down at all," she told Helen.[12]

Louise and Gussie regaled their reporter guest with stories about their colorful neighbor, Pete Lyons, a fellow sheep rancher who "never was above getting a dollar, nor above any method of its getting," according to Helen's reporting.[13] And as the trio came upon a stretch in the dirt trail, they noticed a section of roadway peppered with fresh hoofprints. They spotted a portion of the fence that looked as though it had been mended,

Gussie and Louise. *University of British Columbia, Wallace B. Chung and Madeline H. Chung Collection, "The Girl Ranchers of California," by W. F. Wade.*

and the land on the other side was stripped bare of any vegetation. Even a city slicker like Helen could see the area had been devoured by a hungry herd of something.

"That Pete Lyons pastured his sheep on our land last night," Gussie said.[14]

Every rancher for miles around was well aware of the sheep hotel operated at Jim White's "Ten-Mile Ranch" between Laytonville and Eureka, where a rancher could take his or her herd for a day or two to rest and devour a proper meal from Jim's lush pasture. Of course, he charged for this service—two cents per sheep for twelve hours. The Lahms surmised Pete Lyons had taken advantage of their free grazing pasture rather than board his sheep at the more costly Jim White sheep hotel.

"It means a round-up tonight," Gussie said.[15] So although the women had been in their saddles since early morning, they rounded up the dogs and hired hands and took off into the hills to bring in the entire herd of several thousand sheep. Upon their return the next morning, they counted the animals and came up about a hundred short. This prompted Gussie, with Perro at her side, to saddle up. No one was willing to say where the pair went, but four days later they returned with about a hundred sheep. Just another day in the life of a California rancher.

So as the local politicians in Willits debated the question "Shall a lovely woman be permitted to wear trousers if she needs them in her business?" the Lahm sisters went about their daily chores: roping cattle, mending fences, protecting their sheep from deadly predators, repairing damaged roadways, rounding up strays, and overseeing the ranch hands while managing the business accounts.[16] People said there wasn't a fellow around who was a better judge of cattle, sat firmer in a saddle, or could shoot better than the Lahm girls.

It's not known how the Lahm sisters felt about all the publicity their clothing garnered around the country, but it is worth noting that Helen Grey-Page visited their ranch at an invitation from the women themselves. One thing that is clear: They intended to continue wearing sensible clothes as they went about their daily chores.

According to a report in the *San Francisco Examiner*, they "only ask to be permitted to mind their own business in their own way."[17] The paper added, "[B]ut they say they will wear trousers even if they are not allowed to vote." Some might have wondered if that was a veiled threat to the local politicians in Willits: Beware the day when women vote!

4

Vidal Sisters

"The Girls in the Overalls"

"The first thing you see is a large eight rail horse corral full of horses ranging from the old, broken down cow pony to the wild colt just in from the range. There is some kind of a commotion going on in the corral. . . . An 18-year old girl with a gorgeous pompadour of golden hair has roped a wild horse. . . . She is attired in the regulation chaps and sombrero, but you look at the white shirt waist and the pompadour of gold and wonder."[1]

THE REPORTER FOR THE *CHICAGO TRIBUNE* SEEMED AWESTRUCK BY THE images he described at the Vidal ranch near Gunnison, Colorado, in October 1904: another young woman "sitting calmly in the saddle while a frantic broncho" tried to "throw her up against the clouds"; one in overalls splitting wood with a swing of an ax; two more in a hayfield, one seated on a horse rake, the other on a mower; three more girls stacking alfalfa onto a thirty-foot pile.[2]

Worthy of a feature story splashed across a page of the Chicago newspaper, the chores simply represented a typical day of work for Phillipine "Pearl," Josephine, Methilde "Tillie," Dorothy "Dollie," Bertha, Sophia, Lovina, and Annette Vidal. When their parents died, the sisters and their brother, Robert, had assumed the duties of running the 725-acre ranch. No one seemed surprised that Robert committed to the family business, but when word spread that the eight female siblings were essentially in charge of the operation, it caused a bit of a sensation. No one could

Vidal sisters with horse-drawn hay rake. *Harry H. Buckwalter, History Colorado-Denver, Colorado.*

have predicted that the sisters would become celebrities beyond the local Gunnison community or that they would hold a place in American film history.

~~~

"His case is considered hopeless."[3]

The *Whitehorn News* didn't sugarcoat in reporting the health of Gunnison resident Regis Vidal in May 1901. Suffering from an ailment the paper labeled stomach cancer, the pioneer rancher's future looked dire, and the reports turned out to be accurate. The well-known businessman died, leaving his earthly possessions to his wife, Albine. Ranching had not been without its struggles, and over the years the Vidals had acquired a sizeable debt. Fortunately, Albine was not alone in her determination to save the family enterprise. All nine of her kids stepped up to help.

At the time of Regis's death, Pearl, Josephine, and Methilde were in their early twenties and working in Denver as seamstresses. Dollie, Bertha, Sophia, Lovina, and Annette were still living on the ranch. Annette was only ten, and Dollie, at eighteen, was the oldest of the five living at home. Maybe that's why she was appointed manager of the operation. The family was determined that the ranch would thrive, and they were intent on retiring the debt—$15,000 by some accounts, at 10 percent interest. It was reported that all the female siblings were "sweet, modest girls" and "fine specimens of womanhood."[4] In addition to being "very striking" in appearance, they exhibited the "strength and resolution necessary to meet emergencies and conquer difficulties."[5]

They needed all the strength and resolve they could muster to survive the harsh conditions of their Colorado ranch in the early 1900s. Raising crops and herding cattle on more than seven hundred acres required brute strength as well as business savvy. The older women rotated between working on the ranch and earning much-needed wages in the city. On any given day, the Vidal women could be observed in the fields planting and harvesting crops, tending horses and cattle, milking cows, and carrying water from the well. As winter approached, they prepared for the cold—felling trees with their brother and dragging the trunks from the nearby hills to the ranch, where they used saws and axes to reduce the logs to convenient sizes for the stove. Horses were vital to the operation of the ranch—for riding, pulling wagons and buggies, and most importantly to pull the equipment for the management of the crops. "[E]very girl on the Vidal ranch can go into a bunch of range horses, pick her mount and get him on the end of a rope as well as an expert horseman. They all ride astride, and generally without saddle if in a hurry," according to a news article.[6]

Just three years after Regis's death, Albine died. She had spent some time in a hospital, so those medical expenses added to the family's financial woes. But as time passed, the debt dwindled, and the ranch began to prosper. Local newspapers ran articles about the Vidal women with intriguing headlines: "Girls Run Ranch" and "Daughters Don Trousers and Pay Off Debt." And while their business acumen was recognized, their appearance and clothing often dominated the articles. It was reported the sisters wore overalls—those sturdy, loose-fitting bib trousers worn by farmers as a uniform of sorts—when taming the broncs and cow punching and stacking the voluminous mounds of hay. Intended to protect the wearer's regular clothing from dirt, muck, and other distasteful liquids or solids encountered by a typical rancher during the course of a workday, the overall may not have represented what fashion experts considered chic. But the Vidal sisters found the utilitarian attire perfect for ranch life. "[M]ost women don't know the advantage of wearing trousers," one of the sisters told a reporter. "When the Summer work is over and we don our skirts and go back to Denver we are almost lost for pockets. It's the most aggravating thing you ever saw. When we want our jackknives, or a piece of baling wire, or a short strap, we unconsciously reach for a pocket and then we find we have none."[7] The sisters admitted that a quick inventory of their pockets would reveal monkey wrenches, bits of wire, nails, straps, or jackknives—and the occasional piece of candy.

Much was made of the Vidals' French heritage. Both Regis and Albine were French immigrants, and the family spoke French in their home. It

Tillie in hayfield, Call # CHS-B1032. *Harry H. Buckwalter, History Colorado-Denver, Colorado.*

was reported over and over again that the Vidal sisters wore lacy clothing under their overalls, buckskin gloves to protect their delicate hands, and gold bracelets on their wrists and conducted their day-to-day rituals wearing dainty high-heeled shoes—all because, well, they *were* French. News articles, embellished with pictures of the sisters in their bib overalls, snippets of lace peeking out of the bib or decorative ribbons accentuating the neckline, appeared in newspapers across the country—Chicago and San Francisco—and even internationally in London and Australia.

About the same time the Vidals were gaining notoriety as examples of "what Colorado's young women will do when face to face with seeming crushing difficulties," Denver reporter Harry Buckwalter was transitioning into a career as a filmmaker.[8] By 1902, he had formed a studio called Buckwalter Films, where he produced and directed silent movies. When the plight of the Vidal family caught Harry's attention, he saw it as an opportunity. Somehow, he came into contact with the Vidal sisters and convinced them to star in his short documentary film about life on a Colorado ranch. *The Girls in the Overalls* was distributed by Chicago-based Selig Polyscope Company in October 1904 with Harry as director. The silent black-and-white production was part of the company's Colorado Travelogue series and became one of the earliest western films in America.[9]

Filmed at the Vidal ranch, the production documented the sisters going about their daily routines: sawing and chopping wood, raking and stacking hay, piloting the horse teams as they pulled the rakes and mowers through the fields, jockeying the go-devils (a rake-like contraption that trailed the hay to the barn). It wasn't all drudgery and hard work. Buckwalter posed the family in front of the log ranch house gleefully devouring huge chunks of juicy watermelon for lunch. And he captured the sisters lined up engaging in a rollicking game of leapfrog for an afternoon break. In the final scene of the film, "Fun on a Haystack," the sisters climbed the mountainous pile of hay to slide down the slippery side and land in a heap at the bottom.

The release of *The Girls in the Overalls* in 1904 gave the Vidal family widespread notoriety and invitations from would-be suitors. The sisters were showered with letters from men looking to marry (and acquire

Vidal family. The sisters were not identified in this picture and it is unclear why there were only seven included in the photo. *Harry H. Buckwalter, History Colorado-Denver, Colorado.*

a ranch in Colorado). But the Vidal sisters refused to stray from their pursuit of a debt-free, prosperous family enterprise. "The ranch must be cleared of the mortgage before any of us marries," Dollie was reported to have said.[10]

Long before the release of the film, local suitors had become well aware of the Vidal sisters' priorities. On any Sunday night, six to eight horses could be seen tethered to the hitch rail in front of the ranch house, the young male riders dancing with the sisters in the dining room to the sound of a fiddle or guitar. But visitors knew it was time to depart when the musicians broke into a melody familiar to everyone—"Home Sweet Home." It meant the sisters were ready to slip into their overalls and get back to work. And any young man who might have hoped to continue socializing with the Vidal women knew that "unless he took off his coat and worked in the field" his company was no longer required.[11]

Part III

Law Enforcer, Law Breakers

"About that time there came in my way the literature of a correspondence school which would teach, among other things, short story writing by mail; it set forth all the advantages of a literary career and proposed properly to equip its students in that course for a consideration. This literature I greedily devoured, and felt that I could not let the opportunity slip, though I despaired of getting my husband's consent. I presented the remunerative side of it to him, but he could only see the expense of taking the course, and wondered how I could find time to spend in the preparation, even if it should be profitable in the end; but he believed it was all a humbug; that they would get my money and I would hear from them no more. Contrary to his expectations the school has proven very trustworthy, and I am in the midst of a course of instruction which is very pleasing to me; and I find time for study and exercise between the hours of eight and eleven at night, when the family are asleep and quiet. I am instructed to read a great deal, with a certain purpose in view, but that is impossible, since I had to promise my husband that I would drop all my papers, periodicals, etc., on which I was paying out money for subscription before he would consent to my taking the course. This I felt willing to do, that I might prepare myself for more congenial tasks; I hope to accomplish something worthy of note in a literary way since I have been a failure in all other pursuits."[1]

5

Oklahoma Anderson Noonan

"The Equal of Any Cowboy in the State"[1]

WHEN PROFESSOR GEORGE M. FRIZZELL ANNOUNCED SEVENTH-graders who had perfect attendance in the Tempe Public Schools in November 1899, Oklahoma "Okla" Anderson was at the top of the list. And when he recognized three students who had achieved the highest scholarship in the class, Okla's name made that list, too. Her father at the family ranch in Gila Bend, Arizona, must have been extremely pleased with his youngest daughter. She had been born to John and Lurany Lockhart Anderson in Kansas while the couple waited for the US government to open Oklahoma Territory for homesteaders. The Andersons named their baby in anticipation of the territory being their new home. However, before that could happen, Lurany died, and John headed to Arizona and bought up some land in Gila Bend. It's where Okla grew up and where she learned to ride horses and rope cattle. Tempe was too far for Okla to commute for school, so she likely boarded in the growing town of about a thousand. With its six churches, two hotels, a bank, six general merchandise stores, two livery stables, and three restaurants, in addition to a full mile of graded and graveled streets, Tempe could support a fine public school with enrollment of nearly three hundred students. Even more impressive, there was a territorial normal school—a college specifically for the training of teachers—located in Tempe, and after completing eighth grade, Okla attended a couple years of normal school. It's unclear that she spent any time teaching, but she did become a celebrity of sorts for other accomplishments.

Students at the Tempe college in 1901 when Okla attended. *University Archives Photographs, Arizona State Library.*

Through the Homestead Act and the Desert Land Act of 1877, Okla began to acquire land in 1907 around the Gila Bend area. And when she married into another well-known and prosperous ranching family in the region, her holdings grew. Together with her husband, Daniel Wilson Noonan Jr., she raised cattle, which they marked with their unique brands.

As ranchers in the Arizona Territory, Okla and Dan, like other individuals who dealt in livestock-related enterprises, would have had interactions with the Live Stock Sanitary Board. As law-abiding businessmen and -women, the experiences would have been unremarkable and relatively routine. However, for unlawful individuals, exchanges with the Live Stock Sanitary Board could be unpleasant or even deadly.

Okla's homestead and desert land entries notices. Arizona Republic, *January 15, 1912.*

NOTICE FOR PUBLICATION.
03470

NOTICE FOR PUBLICATION.
04562

31

Okla's brand appeared over the left ribs of her cattle and on the left thigh of her horses. *Brands and Marks of Cattle, Horses, Sheep, Goats and Hogs, Office of the Live Stock Sanitary Board of Arizona.*

Established in 1887 by the territorial legislature, the agency was charged with keeping the territory "free of stock disease and of olden-time range 'rustling.'"[2] It employed detectives, or "livestock inspectors," as they were known, who conducted a variety of duties—inspecting rodeo livestock for ticks, ensuring all livestock brands were recorded, enforcing licensing requirements with butcher shops, and keeping up with the ever-present troublesome rustlers. The Live Stock Sanitary Board appointed individuals to the inspector positions, and they were highly coveted jobs, with monthly salaries of around sixty dollars. In 1915, there were just over eighty inspectors working throughout the territory—all men—until Secretary Sam B. Bradner took the unprecedented step of appointing a female inspector in the Gila Bend district.

Having grown up "in the saddle" and "thoroughly familiar" with the cattle business, Okla was considered an expert at "roping and tying steers" and the "equal of any cowboy in the state."[3] All this meant she was well suited to the rugged duties of livestock inspector. According to the Sanitary Board job description, inspectors were required to be in a saddle from early morning until late at night, and they'd better be prepared for "roughing it in all sorts of weather." A valued livestock inspector needed "cool bravery and good judgement." But most importantly, the job required a person who could handle a six-gun, as "true marksmanship" was often required to tame a particularly notorious rustler. The inspectors' duties could be daunting, as every shipment of cattle in the district required the inspector to count the animals and examine their brands. Okla's hours in the saddle as a young girl prepared her well for her new job as she wandered the acres of range, picking up mavericks (unbranded animals) and "running down rumors of illegal operations." According to newspaper accounts, Okla was adept at catching rustlers "red-handed in the act of altering a brand" and delivering them to the local justices of the peace.[4]

In the fall of 1917, Okla found herself in a legal tussle with a fellow whom she claimed rustled a couple of her horses from the open range near the Noonan ranch. By some accounts, W. W. Bruner was simply a "rosy-faced, gray-haired, middle-aged gentleman, with a mild blue eye that looks at you kindly through silver rimmed spectacles" who got caught up in a misunderstanding.[5] In the court proceedings that ensued after Okla's charges of rustling, Bruner claimed he had indeed taken the wandering horses from the open range and brought them to a corral in Phoenix for safekeeping but that he never intended to keep them for himself. The corral attendant testified that Bruner told him they weren't his horses and that they would be boarded only for a few days. The courthouse was packed with local cattlemen who were eager to learn the outcome of the case. Despite Bruner's claim that he had no felonious intent in taking the horses, the spectators showed little compassion for anyone who took animals from the open range. And Okla, the alleged victim of the crime as well as a law enforcer for the Sanitary Board, became an "energetic and ready witness" at the trial—determined to see justice done. When Bruner's attorney asked if she believed the defendant intended to keep the horses for his own use, she replied, "Yes, I thought he did." Okla added that she hoped the courts would find Bruner guilty of the theft and "advise him to rove, travel, and get out of the country."[6] However, the presiding justice dismissed the charges.

Okla's supervisors were very pleased with Arizona's first female livestock inspector and said they anticipated hiring additional women. "In the future it is likely that women will supersede men entirely in this work," the board's Sam Bradner said.[7] And four years after Okla had been hired, a representative of the Live Stock Sanitary Board said in an interview that he was very proud of Okla's accomplishments and wished that he had more inspectors as efficient as she. He said he was eager to hire any woman who was skilled with a revolver and experienced "in the use of a rope at the gallop."[8]

6

Emma L. Watson

"Smoothest Woman in the Country"

"Many Are Indicted for Conspiracy in Land Frauds"[1]

NEWSPAPERS ACROSS THE COUNTRY IN 1905 SCREAMED SIMILAR HEAD-lines about the sensational situation unfolding in Oregon—a long and tangled trail of bribes, lies, and scams involving "some low-down rascals and High-up citizens."[2] Some of the most prominent issued statements: "I am in no way involved in these frauds," congressman and commissioner of the General Land Office Binger Hermann proclaimed. And this from Senator John H. Mitchell: "That is an infernal lie."[3] Even the wife of one of the alleged conspirators had something to say about the outrageous accusations against her husband, Stephen Puter: "I am positive ... that the Government is in the wrong.... I know that my husband will be exonerated when he has had his trial."[4] However, Mrs. Puter turned out to be wrong about her husband, the "king of the Oregon land sharks," who ended up serving time for his role in the scheme to defraud the government.[5] And while Mrs. Puter claimed, "I know so little about my husband's business," Mr. Puter had teamed up with another woman to execute his shaky business practices and sustain his fraudulent enterprise.[6]

By some accounts, Emma Watson was a poor widow trying to survive in challenging circumstances, but the US government described her as a woman who "knowingly, unlawfully, wickedly, and corruptly conspired to defraud the United States out of its title to certain public lands by means of false, fraudulent, and fictitious" practices.[7] The indictments of Emma and a web of other individuals stemmed from the sale of lands in Oregon that were intended for public lands. And by the end of the years-long investigations, the federal government had uncovered a "generation of wholesale fraud in the expropriation of the public lands."[8]

Everybody wanted the precious land making up the great American Northwest. By the early 1900s in Oregon, homesteaders, timber enterprises, and the federal government as well as other interests, such as railroads and ranchers, fought over the ownership of the thickly forested acres. There was money to be made in a variety of ways, and Stephen Puter set out to get his share of the riches, even if it meant working around the laws governing land ownership. Emma Watson stepped up to help or unknowingly got suckered in—depending on which version of facts one chose to believe.[9]

From 1904 to 1906, Emma's life became a roller-coaster ride of indictments, court appearances, grand jury interviews, pursuit by federal agents, legal wrangles, a trial, and finally jail time. By the early 1900s, plenty of people had taken up the government's offer of land ownership provided by the Homestead Act of 1862, which allowed individuals to acquire 160 acres by making improvements to the land—building a dwelling and cultivating the land for five years. While Oregon wasn't the only place where unscrupulous individuals abused the homestead laws, Emma Watson stepped into a highly well-organized system of graft and fraud when she agreed to put her name (as well as an alias, Emma Porter) on applications for her 160-acre plot—at least a dozen times. While Puter was the mastermind, she was a small cog in his machine, which included a trip to the nation's capital in February 1902 to entice Oregon's Senator John Mitchell to pressure the local Portland land office to speed up steps for completing the claims process. Puter invited Emma, who was "made up as a handsome, helpless widow," to meet with Senator Mitchell, who had represented Oregon for years.[10] It was believed the senator would respond well to an attractive woman who presented herself as a damsel in distress. She had invested a great deal of money in the land deals and needed to recoup her investments as quickly as possible. To bolster Emma's sorrowful story, Puter and Emma dropped a couple of $1,000 bills behind with the senator as they departed—something Puter later included in his tell-all book written from his jail cell after the sordid conspiracy was exposed.

Puter and his partner, Horace Greeley McKinley, had been conducting their disreputable business for a few years, gobbling up land meant for honest homesteaders—through bogus claims—just to turn around and sell fraudulently acquired land to unsuspecting individuals or to other business interests. At the same time, the federal government intended to reserve some of the lands that Puter was acquiring through Emma and other claimants' bogus homesteading applications. The law pertaining to public domain entitled the government to remove private citizens from these lands by offering the homesteaders compensation. This land grab by the federal government put a crimp in Puter's business, and as the government started looking into some of the roadblocks to acquiring the lands, it became obvious that Puter was one of those barriers that needed investigating.

A photographer was hired to snap pictures of the homesteads (known as "strawberry patches") where Emma and others swore they were living and mak-

Emma Watson. *From* Looters of the Public Domain, *by S. A. D. Puter and Horace Stevens, 1907.*

ing improvements.[11] It very quickly became obvious that Emma and the others were less than honest. No one could farm the claims—they were located on mountaintops, where snow covered the ground well into June, and some were on inaccessible mountain peaks or on the sides of steep cliffs. A picture of Emma's strawberry patch clearly showed densely tree-covered land above the snow level, and there were no signs of a dwelling.[12]

As things heated up and investigators started closing in on Puter and his ring of defrauders, people became edgy. Plenty of dishonest people had reason to worry: land office investigators who accepted bribes to falsely issue favorable reports about the unimproved homestead claims, the timberland broker who purchased fraudulently obtained claims, the US attorney who tried to derail the work of an honest government prosecutor, the judge who adjusted shady accounting practices to protect his law partner who happened to be a US senator. High-ranking officials issued statements claiming innocence or, if that didn't sound plausible, ignorance. When Puter was indicted in October 1903 and it looked as though he would go to trial for his misdeeds, some of his accomplices who could serve as witnesses for the prosecutors disappeared. His partner, McKinley, fled to China, where he was reportedly making a living as a roulette dealer in a gambling establishment.

Emma was one of those who couldn't be found. Government investigators hired a "shadow," detective "Dug" Doyle, to "rope" ("locate and fetch, without arresting") Emma.[13] And in April 1904, Emma was located shortly after the feds had issued indictments for her. According to newspaper reports, federal agents considered Emma the "smoothest woman in the country" for having eluded investigators for months. And when they found her in a Chicago boardinghouse by tailing Puter and enlisting the cooperation of her landlady, agents approached with a "not over-gentle knock upon her door," to which she "acquiesced with charming grace." Although she considered the intrusion by the authorities a "little rude," Emma calmly responded, "What can I do for you?"[14] When the government agent explained he had a warrant for her arrest, she calmly replied, "All right, I will go with you."[15]

If newspaper accounts could be believed, she asked the agents to give her a little time to don proper attire before accompanying them to the local jail, after which she emerged wearing an elegant gown with priceless gems dripping from her arms. Other accounts called the fashion-related stories ludicrous. Reports from the Dearborn Street Jail indicated Emma was as "uncommunicative as the Sphinx" when reporters tried to lure her into conversation.[16] Even government agents failed to get much out of her despite being "sweated by some of the best detectives in the service."[17]

On April 4, 1904, Emma was arraigned in a Chicago courtroom and the same day boarded a train with a US deputy marshal. One of the federal agents who had been trying to locate Emma for months warned the Chicago authorities, "Don't overlook the shackles," as they transported her to the courtroom and the train station.[18] He warned that Puter and other accomplices "will have her off that train in a jiffy, even if they have to hold it up."[19] Rumors had been floating around that there would be an attempt to rescue her, so the marshal was heavily armed with revolvers, and as an added precaution, the name of the train was tightly guarded. But reporters approached Emma, who was supposedly dressed in an expensive hat and patent-leather boots, and pressed her to make a statement. "The secret agents have told their side of the story. I will not tell mine until I reach Portland," she said. "The secret service agents may have said too much for their own good. That's all."[20]

Arriving in Portland, Emma, "[w]ith a look of supreme indifference on her face," was booked into the Multnomah County Jail but was set free with a $4,000 bond and set up residence at the Imperial Hotel.[21] She was arraigned in a federal courtroom on May 2, charged with conspiracy to defraud the government of lands. Pleading not guilty, she waived the reading of the indictment, and the trial was set for May 18, 1904.

Imperial Hotel, Portland, Oregon, 1906. *Brück & Sohn, Wikipedia, Creative Commons.*

However, it wasn't until November that the case went to trial in Portland. Some of the evidence presented sealed Emma's fate—a surveyor who testified she had presented him with a $250 bribe and a handwriting expert who declared the same person had signed a homestead claim "Emma Porter" and "Emma Watson."

In December 1904, Puter, Emma, and others were found guilty. However, as investigations related to the massive land fraud endeavor continued, Emma and Puter were released and continued to provide prosecutors with vital information leading to indictments and eventual convictions of additional gang members, including Senator Mitchell, in July 1905. A variety of circumstances contributed to the downfall of the senator; spelling errors made by a young stenographer attempting to cover up the senator's illegal practices was one of the more laughable. At the direction of the senator and a dishonest judge who had been a partner with the senator, the stenographer—who happened to be the judge's son—wrote up a fake contract to pass off as an original, at the same time destroying an original incriminating contract. In the doctored contract, the stenographer spelled *salary* "salery" and *constituent* "constituant."[22] When a grand jury asked three stenographers who had written up the original contract to spell the two words, they did so correctly. When they asked the judge's son to spell them, he again misspelled the words—one of several indications that the second document was a fraud.

Federal prosecutors were highly displeased about leaks from a secret grand jury in which Emma provided them with damaging information about Mitchell and others. Determined to find the source of the leaks, agents began to shadow jury members. Puter confessed to some of the crimes he was accused of and worked with prosecutors. When he was indicted for additional crimes, federal agents arrested him in Boston in March 1906. It did not go smoothly, as Puter pulled a revolver on the arresting agent and fled. After a cross-country search, he was apprehended in Alameda, California, before he could make his getaway to China. In June, Emma was brought to the Multnomah County Jail in Portland, where Puter was being held. She had been living in the San Francisco area and claimed she'd survived the April 18 earthquake but lost all her possessions in the subsequent fires. She expressed surprise at her capture

Stephen Puter writing in his jail cell. *Photo is the property of Oregonian Publishing Co.*

by authorities, saying had she known they were looking for her, she would have traveled to Portland at their request. At 2:00 p.m. on July 6, 1906, Puter appeared in court and was sentenced to two years in the Multnomah County Jail, where he wrote *Looters of the Public Domain*, his book describing his exploits as "King of the Oregon Land Fraud Ring."[23] Meanwhile, Emma, who had never been sentenced for her 1904 conviction, remained in her Multnomah County Jail cell, furnished with a bed, a mattress, two chairs, a wooden washstand, a tin basin, and a small mirror.

As the investigations resulted in more indictments over the next months, some thanks to Emma's inside knowledge, she remained in the county jail, serving as a model prisoner and at times filling in duties that typically would have been the duties of a matron. The jail staff found her "humanitarian instincts" especially useful in dealing with "insane women."[24] There were reports that, because government prosecutors perceived Emma a minor player in the overall scheme and because some believed she had been unaware of the deviousness of her actions related to the fraudulent activities, she was given great liberties in the jail—only being confined to a cell at night.

Few were surprised when on September 19, 1906, a "nattily attired" woman in a "light grey plaid traveling suit," her face hidden behind a "pink automobile veil," emerged from the jail accompanied by a US marshal to the nearby federal court building, where she signed a recognizance bond and walked out of the building a free woman. No longer needed as a witness and with scores of individuals, including a judge, government officials, and politicians, either under indictment or convicted, Emma, her head held high, stopped to smell the flowers and shrubs in the yard. Despite the heavy veil, reporters maintained her "prison pallor" was noticeable as she walked away. It was also noted, "Not a friend was there to greet her."[25]

7

Emma Bell

Montana Rustler

As deputy sheriff in Cascade County, Montana, in 1902, Dennis Lennihan was called on to deal with a wide variety of unruly citizens: an eleven-year-old boy who terrorized his friends and threatened to cut their hearts out if they refused his demands, a gun-brandishing man who treated a group of friends to free drinks at the saloon but refused to pay at the end of the night, a local baker who used indecent language in the presence of women and children. All part of the job for the lawman. So when neighboring Deputy Sheriff Ed Hogan asked Lennihan to help out in a cattle-rustling investigation, he was happy to oblige.

On Tuesday, June 24, ranchers William Snow and Mandus Hinderager were out on the range for roundup when they passed a neighbor's ranch and spotted a cow owned by Snow. And while Snow recognized his cow, he didn't see the calf that he remembered the cow had produced in February. It all seemed mighty suspicious to the ranchers, and they headed into Great Falls to report their findings to Deputy Sheriff Hogan, who asked Lennihan to visit Byerdorf and Nollar, the local slaughterhouse. Lennihan immediately learned that a man and woman had sold three calves to the establishment on Monday evening, June 23. It didn't take long for Deputies Hogan and Lennihan to learn Emma Bell and her hired man, Earl Davis, were responsible for the theft of the animals. Emma, whom it was said "rides the range like any cowboy" and "could rope, throw, and brand like a man," already had a bit of a reputation in the county—she was on her third husband and had been suspected of cattle rustling a few years earlier.[1] The sheriff handed over the evidence to county attorney A. C. Gormley, and a warrant for the arrest of Emma and Earl was issued. By eleven o'clock on the night of June 28, the two prisoners were locked up in the county jail.

At her arraignment Emma, represented by James W. Freeman, pled not guilty to a charge of grand larceny and was released on a $500 bond. Mr. Freeman took the opportunity to set the record straight by informing the court that those rumors about his client previously being accused of cattle rustling were inaccurate. It was true that her former husband had been tried for rustling, but Emma was simply a witness in the case.

By the end of July, Emma was back in a Fort Benton courthouse. William Snow testified that when he spotted his cow at the Bell ranch, she "acted as though she had lost her calf." And when he asked Emma about the situation, she had claimed she sold a calf to a Great Falls butcher a few days before but that it belonged to her. Snow testified (and it was substantiated by other witnesses) that he had conducted an experiment of taking his cow to the slaughterhouse to meet the calf, which immediately ran to the cow, proving that it was the calf's mother and that it belonged to Snow. When Emma testified, she explained that her hired man, Earl Davis, was at fault. Yes, she had sold calves to Byerdorf and Nollar, but Earl had accidentally loaded the neighbors' calves onto the Bell wagon. She said she "supposed that he knew enough to take calves belonging to her," but she shouldn't have put her trust in Earl. And as far as the calf seeking out its mother, neighbor Myron Brown testified that Emma told him, "If I stole a calf, don't you think that I would have sense enough to drive the d— cow away?"[2] The prosecution commenced to prove that Emma had indeed driven the cow away from its calf so she and Earl could easily load it up and take it to the slaughterhouse.

Earl, who was out on bail, took the stand and explained that Emma had in fact gone to the corral with him when he loaded the calves. He provided detail about her showing him how to load the calves by propping an old door against the end of the ranch wagon to create an incline for the calves to walk up. The case went to the jury at nine the night of July 29 after each side had given about an hour and a half of testimony. The next day, the jury returned with a conviction—something that made

Emma Bell's mug shot. *[PAc 85-91 01270], Montana Historical Society Research Center Photograph Archives, Helena, Montana.*

local stockmen, who had gathered at the courthouse and who had a great aversion to stock rustlers, very happy. When the verdict was read, a local newspaper reported that Emma fainted and had to be taken to the jailer's house for the night. Reporting on the conviction, a Butte newspaper predicted that Emma would "no doubt find herself cramped within the stone walls of the prison." And that she "will miss the wild free life of her prairie home while cogitating on the past within the confines of deer lodge."[3]

On Saturday, August 9, Sheriff Charles Crawford transported Emma and two male prisoners to the state prison at Deer Lodge, where the two men would serve one year each for grand larceny and manslaughter. Emma's three-year sentence for grand larceny may have seemed excessive to some—but not to W. G. Downing, who had helped prosecute her for the local cattlemen's association. On the overnight trip to the prison, Sheriff Crawford allowed Emma to stay at a hotel to avoid an "introduction to the low criminal element" she would encounter at the local jail.[4] However, there was no avoiding her new home at the "home of the wicked" at Deer Lodge.

At the time of Emma's incarceration, the prison was managed by a private enterprise, Conley and McTague, which was paid forty-five cents per day for each inmate. If an interview given by one of the inmates during an inspection could be believed, the company was doing a superb job. "No landlord at a first-class hotel could be more attentive to the comfort of his guests than are the contractors of the Deer Lodge prison," the prisoner claimed.[5] And shortly before Emma arrived to join a handful of women inmates, the company had completed some changes related to the handling of female prisoners.

Previously, the male deputy warden had been in charge of the women prisoners. In 1901, the first matron, Frances Panghorn, had been hired. A graduate of the Michigan State Training School for Nurses, with four years' work in charitable institutions, Frances was considered a favorable choice for the Montana prison. She joined the prison after holding the position of superintendent at a hospital in Warm Springs, Montana. Frances immediately instituted new policies for the women inmates at Deer Lodge: dark blue uniforms for all and lessons in cooking and sewing, in addition to long walks outside the prison walls—all intended to

Deer Lodge prison. *Powell County Museum and Arts Foundation, Deer Lodge, Montana.*

instill usefulness rather than idleness in the female inmates. When Frances resigned in October 1902, Kate Leonard was hired as matron. But a year later, Kate resigned to become a bookkeeper in Hamilton, Montana. Not long after, Emma also left Deer Lodge.

After eighteen months at the prison, Emma was granted a pardon by Governor Joseph K. Toole. In her petition for release, she wrote, "I have now been in the penitentiary a little more than 18 months and pray you to grant me a pardon, as I have an aged mother who depends wholly upon me for support, she being entirely alone while I am here. I assure you that in the future I shall endeavor to lead an honest, straightforward life in all things, and will give you no further trouble." Her petition was supported by the prison contractors Conley and McTague, who wrote, "The way we are fixed to take care of female prisoners in this place, one year on a woman is harder than five on a man, therefore we would like to see her pardoned." Special counsel W. G. Downing, who had helped in prosecuting Emma, also put in a good word for her. The governor stated that he had "no doubt that her punishment has been effectual and that the ends of justice have been fully subserved."[6] When the state board of pardons met in Helena on February 9, 1904, James Donovan, president of the board, adopted the application for a pardon, reading, "Whereas, the governor of Montana has this day officially notified this board that he has granted diminution of sentence by pardon . . . to one Emma Bell—Case No. 1120."[7] Earl Davis never was charged, as there wasn't enough evidence supporting his role in the crime.

Part IV

Growers

"The addition of two children to our family never altered or interfered with the established order of things. . . . I still hoed and tended the truck patches and garden, still watered the stock and put out feed for them, still went to the hay field and helped harvest the golden grain later on when the cereals ripened; often took one team and dragged ground to prepare the seed-bed for wheat. . . . I put up canned goods for future use; gather in many bushels of field beans and the other crops usually raised on the farm; make sour-kraut, ketchup, pickles, etc."[1]

"In early spring we are planting potatoes, making plant beds, planting garden, early corn patches, setting strawberries, planting corn, melons, cow peas, sugar cane, beans, popcorn, peanuts. . . . Later in June we harvest clover hay, in July timothy hay, and in August pea hay. Winter wheat is ready to harvest the latter part of June, and oats the middle of July."[2]

8

Emily Lofland Roberson

Woman with a Deficient Obituary

WHEN EMILY LOFLAND ROBERSON DIED IN THE SUMMER OF 1943, HER husband, Joseph Roberson, had been dead more than fifty years. Yet a good portion of *her* obituary published in the *Berkeley* (California) *Daily Gazette* was devoted to *his* accomplishments as an employee of Wells, Fargo, and Company and Russell, Majors, and Waddell (the company that started the Pony Express). The writer of Emily's obituary even managed to squeeze in a few lines about her uncle, a pioneer of Monterey, California, who had traveled over the Santa Fe Trail. As was the tradition, Emily's club and church memberships were mentioned, as were her offspring. Not a word about her celebrity as a rancher, olive grower, and winner of numerous awards at state and local citrus fairs as well as an international exposition while raising two daughters.

Emily grew up in Tennessee, where her dad was a politician, and she attended the Memphis female college, earning a diploma in literature and history. A local newspaper described Emily and her classmates on graduation day as a "bouquet of twenty beautiful young ladies, who looked as if carved out of purest snow and dipped in rose-juice."[1] On that June day in 1873, her classmates would not have predicted that Emily would one day become proprietor of "one of the largest and most successful fruit ranches in the Sierra foothills of California."[2]

After her marriage in 1878 to Joseph Roberson, the couple lived in California, where he invested in stage lines and railroads and completed a manuscript for a book about the Pony Express. When Joseph died in

50

1888, leaving Emily with two young daughters, she purchased a property known as the Gould Ranch, a few miles outside Auburn, California. Her parents and siblings thought it an improper endeavor for a lady, but she refused to allow those sentiments to sidetrack her ambitions. The previous owners of her property had established fruit and olive trees and even a few tea plants. By the spring of 1889, Emily had added twenty acres of olives and peaches. Overall, she had about 5,000 fruit trees and 1,500 olive trees, and the tea plants were thriving. Emily favored Picholine olives, introduced to California from France, for their palatable taste and large oil production, and the Rubra, another producer of superior-quality oil. Also from France, the Oblonga was delightful as a pickled product; other varieties found at Emily's Olivina Farm were Manzanillo, Pendulier, and Nevadillo from Spain.

Emily constantly read the latest information available about fruit growing. "I have felt so ignorant and it has all been so new to me that I am anxious to profit by other people's experience," she said.[3] A savvy businesswoman, she marketed her ripe and pickled olives; pressed and packaged olive oil; and, after seeing the demand for olive trees in the state, established a nursery, selling olive trees and cuttings to other growers. It was rumored that a nurseryman had offered Emily a hundred dollars for one of her Rubra trees, which he wanted to use to start cuttings. Barely a year after Emily had set up her business, the *Sacramento Bee* wrote, "The oil from this place ranks with the best producer in the state. . . . [T]his year the product will largely exceed that of any previous pressing."[4]

The following year was a challenging one for Emily, when "unprece-dented" winter storms delayed the harvest and marauding robins swooped down from the mountains devouring much of her crop—up to ten thou-sand pounds by some estimates.[5] It was a blow to her hopes for a bumper crop. She was disappointed with her two acres of ten-year-old trees yield-ing only one hundred gallons of oil—worth a discouraging $600 in the marketplace. However, the setbacks did not prevent Emily from show-casing her olives and olive oil at the Northern Citrus Fair in Marysville in January 1891, where that part of the state "Wears Her Golden Girdle of Fruits" with pride, according to the *Sacramento Daily Record-Union*.[6] While Emily and one neighbor, a raisin and Smyrna fig grower, were the

Emily Roberson's tea plant, 1902. *Courtesy of the California History Room, California State Library, Sacramento, California.*

only two individuals representing Placer County at the event, growers from around the area took advantage of the opportunity to promote their products through delightfully intriguing displays: oranges, lemons, and wines made from grapes grown in the Marysville vicinity; entire buildings constructed from northern California fruits; a cottage's gable ends overlaid with oranges, the chimney and roof wrapped in red apples; a full-rigged ship, its hull sheathed with prunes, its cargo mountains of citrus fruits. And the talk of the gala: fruit from the "Bidwell Bar Tree," thought to be the oldest orange tree in northern California (planted in 1856 in Oroville and producing more than two thousand oranges each year).[7]

At the California State Citrus Fair in January 1892, Emily's ripe olives and pickled olives each took first place in their categories, with $25 and $20 premiums paid to her. Her olive oil took first place, paying a $50 premium. Emily's popcorn took second place, paying a $1 premium; her tea plant took first, paying $2.50; and her third-place plums paid $2.50. One of the directors of the State Agricultural Society, which sponsored the citrus fair, applauded Emily's efforts: "The pickled ripe olives exhibited by Mrs. Emily Roberson at the Auburn Fair are the most delicate table relish ever seen in this state. A prominent hotel keeper of the bay district said they were too nice; they would be eaten altogether too greedily for wholesome profit to his business." He was just as impressed with her oil: "And the samples of oil exhibited by the same lady, when put in comparison with a bottle that was at the Paris Exposition, and there received the highest award, was found so identical with it that in a test made without knowledge of either the difference could not be detected."[8]

By the close of the 1892 harvest, Emily reported a successful season. Her three-acre grove with three hundred, eleven-year-old trees had produced twenty thousand pounds of olives. And each tree produced three to four gallons of oil, which she sold at $5 per gallon. Receipts for the three acres totaled about $4,500.

Emily's 160-acre Olivina Farm had been only partially cultivated when she bought it, but she worked steadily at "subjecting the woodland and the chaparral to the ax," clearing land for her precious olives and other fruits—oranges, apples, apricots, cherries, plums, and grapes. She had experimented with other crops and after some consideration became committed to replacing her peaches with Japanese persimmons. "It is a tree that comes into bearing quickly; it yields heavily; and the fruit brings a very high price," Emily explained.[9] "As yet the market is rather limited, but the demand is growing."

There never seemed to be any downtime for Emily, as her assorted products ripened at

Persimmon fruit. *Library of Congress, LC-DIG-jpd-01223.*

different times of the year. Summer and fall saw the picking, packing, and hauling of fruits. Then the olives were ready for harvesting and pressing. Weeding, pruning, and spraying were never-ending tasks. She was a hands-on grower, supervising a team of ten men. However, she wasn't hesitant to get her hands dirty, too, at times boxing fruit for shipment. "I do not allow a box of fruit of any kind to go away without myself inspecting it and making sure that it is all right," she said.[10]

Her reading, combined with a few years' experience under her belt, made Emily open to new ideas and techniques for shrinking expenses. "I have heretofore sold through the fruit companies, but I think I can sell direct to eastern purchasers with great advantage and without much more trouble. This year I shall do my own shipping, both of oil and fruit. And I hope that I shall make it succeed," she said.[11]

And then there was the California Midwinter Exposition—a mini world's fair of sorts—held in San Francisco in 1894 for six months. The fair opened on January 27 in Golden Gate Park, where "wonders of the world" were on display and "creative genius of the century" would "find the utmost appreciation."[12] At the Agriculture and Horticulture Building, designed by Samuel Newsom at a cost of $58,000, Emily and other growers granted visitors from across the globe a glimpse into their lives in a "land of sunshine, fruit and flowers," with its "sea of billowing grains"; foothills resembling "tawny lions slumbering in the palpitating heat"; and "thousands of acres" of vineyards, peaches, apricots, and almond and olive groves.[13] When awards were announced at the fair, the General Arthur cigar manufactured by Kerbs, Wertheim, and Schiffer took first place over its competitors. Main and Winchester took first place for the artistic display of its harnesses, saddles, and whips. And three of the five brands of lager beer manufactured by the John Wieland Brewery and exhibited by the California Bottling Company won top honors. First-place award for the best olive oil at the exposition was awarded to . . .

There was a bit of confusion regarding this prize. Initially it was announced that the first-place award for olive oil went to J. L. Howland of the Howland Brothers firm in Pomona. It's possible the judges had been influenced by the donation of a beautiful cut-glass globe containing two gallons of Howland Brothers' olive oil just a few days before the exposition opening. Or perhaps they had been overly impressed with Howland's showy display—an eighteen-foot-high tower of four hundred olive oil bottles. But soon after the initial announcement of Howland's victory, a follow-up news story set the record straight. "Efforts are to be made to place the credit where it properly belongs," the *Placer Herald* announced, "with Mrs. Emily Roberson," whose "tasty showing" from her orchards in fact had taken first place. And the newspaper promised, "As soon as Commissioner Madden" could "get around to it," he intended to correct the "false impression" created by the previous announcement related to Mr. Howland.[14]

In November 1902, the Northern California Citrus Fair was held in San Francisco and sponsored by the State Board of Trade. Each day of the event recognized a different group—University of California Day, Stanford Day, and a special day set aside by the boards of education of San Francisco and Oakland for schoolchildren to learn about the geography of the state. Principals dismissed classes at 1:00 p.m. to allow children to view the exhibits, after which they were required to write a composition. Kids as well as adults certainly were fascinated by some of the sights— two mammoth pumpkins weighing in at 148 pounds (one with a drawing

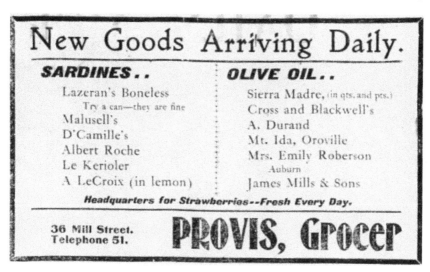

Advertisement for Emily's products. Morning Union *(Grass Valley, California)*, May 4, 1901.

of a map of Kern County indicating the locations of the oil fields) and a nine-foot stalk of alfalfa grown from a seed. And tea drinkers were not alone in their admiration for Emily's "full-grown blossoming tea plant" coming from the "only tea plantation which exists in the State."[15] The three-foot-tall plant, bearing several branches and blossoms of white petals surrounding yellow stamens, caused a sensation.

By the time of Emily's death in 1943, her accomplishments and contributions to California's citrus industry were remarkable. Unfortunately, her obituary failed to mention any of them.

9

Amanda Ida Watkins

"A Blizzard of a Woman"

LONG BEFORE THE *NEW YORK TIMES* LABELED AMANDA IDA WATKINS A "blizzard of a woman" for her outspokenness in a congressional investigation in 1932, she was highly regarded for her business savvy as a cattle and wheat rancher in Oklahoma and Kansas. Having built a reputation first as a "cattle queen" in Oklahoma and then as the "Wheat Queen" of Kansas, Ida, as she was widely known, had little regard for the words of those city slickers in New York City.[1]

She had arrived in Kansas by covered wagon as a child with her parents in 1875; taught school for a time; and married Joel D. Watkins, a cattle rancher in Oklahoma Territory. When he died in 1902, Ida carried on the cattle enterprise, earning her designation as a cattle queen as she "rode the range and trail with the cowboys, helped rope and brand calves, punched cattle." In 1910, she decided to sell out her cattle business and retire to Garden City, Kansas. "I thought I'd done my share of all the hard work in the world," she said at the time. Cattle punching behind her and a little money in her pocket from the sale of her cattle ranch, Ida bought a half section of land near Sublette, in Haskell County, Kansas, for $3,500 and put a renter on it with the condition that he plant two hundred acres in wheat. They shared the profits at the end of the season, and she came away with more than $8,000. The impressive return on her investment caused Ida to reconsider her retirement. "I found that loafing was the hardest work I had ever done," she said. And that's when she decided to become a wheat farmer. By 1928, Ida owned more than four thousand acres of land and had earned the title "Wheat Queen of Kansas."[2]

"Well, if I'm queen of anything I'm the queen of hard work," Ida said. Her day started at four in the morning with breakfast and then out to the fields, where teams of workers worked in three, eight-hour shifts at crucial stages—such as harvest time. As many as seven combines and tractors were kept going as the workers ate in shifts. Meals were prepared in the house and transported to the fields, so the men wasted little time. They were served hot food and steaming coffee laid out on clean table-cloths, with the running boards of cars and trucks as their dining tables. The machinery was never idle, as the workers ate in relays. Ida's workers were paid even on days when the weather kept them from going to the fields; tractor and truck drivers earned five dollars per day, while combine operators got eight dollars. Ida supervised the workers, but she also operated the equipment as efficiently as the male workers, even when it came to repairs. "I can handle a monkey wrench or hammer as well as I can a mixing bowl or carving knife," she remarked.[3] And observers compared Ida's operation to a "metropolitan factory" adapted to agriculture, applying "big business methods to agriculture."[4]

Ida's entrepreneurial spirit produced notable rewards. In 1926, she harvested fifty thousand bushels of wheat from two thousand acres, making her a profit of $75,000—more than the president of the United States at the time.[5] She wasn't shy about sharing her financial successes, showing a newspaper reporter her accounting records. "Here is the record of 280 acres of land here in Haskell County that I bought in 1923. There's the purchase price, $7,200 in cash, or a trifle over $25.50 an acre," she said in a 1928 interview. "In four years I sold for cash $28,000 worth of wheat off that one tract. . . . In what other business can you show me such a profit?"[6]

She was eager to credit the Kansas soil for the productivity of wheat growing in the "old short-grass country"—several counties in southwest Kansas where the prairies had been covered with "short, curly buffalo grass."[7] She boasted that many farmers who had begun farming in the region had become quite successful over time simply by working hard. "Hard work, mixed with common sense, never starved to death on a Kansas farm," she said.[8]

However, for some farmers and ranchers, hard work and good sense were no match for mother nature and a crippling economy. When the stock market crashed in 1929 and the economic downturn that became known as the Great Depression set in, ranchers and farmers were deeply affected. The 1920s and 1930s were filled with challenges as the nation fell into economic depression and the Dust Bowl swept the land. During World War I (1914–1918) the demand for farm products, such as wheat, was high. When the war ended, the demand shrunk, and farmers were left with surpluses, which led to plummeting prices for the growers. Throughout the 1920s farmers experienced roller-coaster conditions. Many farmers and ranchers had gone into debt in the 1920s. When crop prices fell, they were not able to pay their loans to the banks. As more and more farmers and ranchers defaulted on loans, banks closed. The devastating economy coupled with episodes of drought took a toll.

Ida, along with her fellow ranchers, was affected by the uncertainty. Ida had a bumper crop in 1928, but she had built new granaries to house it. A *Kansas City Star* reporter found her "creeping on her hands and knees" from one of the storage structures "running over with 20,000 bushels of golden wheat." Shaking the wheat from her skirt and stockings, "as one shakes off the snowflakes in a winter storm," Ida told the visitor, "I harvested 50,000 bushels this year, and ... every bushel of it in storage here on my place. I won't sell a grain for less than $1 a bushel."[9]

In 1929, President Herbert Hoover set up a Federal Farm Board meant to stabilize falling farm prices.[10] Among other aims, it encouraged growers to store their surplus products until the demand increased. Initially, Ida was open to the idea. "It's not right to throw all this wheat on the market. I'm storing a lot of mine," she said.[11] She believed that she and her fellow ranchers needed to give the government agency a chance to prove itself. But by 1931, Ida's patience had expired. She and other growers blamed government policies for a "diminishing in the movement of new wheat."[12]

And in 1932, Congress had heard enough complaints about the Farm Board and other government agencies to justify an investigation. A special committee of Congress was formed to "investigate Government competition with private enterprise," and more than $13,000 was appropriated

Amanda Watkins's wheat farm was affected by government programs. *A 1932 Herblock Cartoon, © The Herb Block Foundation.*

for the project.[13] Over a period of eight months, more than six hundred witnesses from a wide spectrum of industries—hotel and restaurant, lumber, envelope manufacturers, bands and musical groups, architects, and others—were called to testify under oath. One was Ida, who traveled to Kansas City to give the committee her perspective about the Farm Board. "I know you will be interested in hearing our plea that this deplorable situation in large measure was brought about by Government interference,"

Ida told the assembled group of officials in explaining the effects of government influence on grain markets.[14] "We did not ask the Congress of the United States to adopt the principles of socialism and communism that it has in the Farm Board," she said. "Government has no place in our business. Leave us alone. We want open, competitive markets for the disposition of our products."[15]

As for the continued role of the Farm Board, Ida had this to say about the "doggone, damnable Government interference" of the board: "I want them to keep out of our business. I want them to kick the devil out of them and get them out of here. That is what I want."[16]

Ida's testimony prompted a Kansas newspaper to brand her a "militant Kansas widow," while the *New York Times* fixed the "Blizzard of a Woman" label on her as well as issued a warning to politicians to "Walk wide o' the Widow at Sublette."[17] Still, the *Times* commended Ida, a rancher "tired of producing wheat at prices which the Farm Board has been so powerful in sustaining," as a witness who "speaks from the heart," having seen many of her fellow ranchers foreclosed on.[18] And ultimately, the role of the Farm Board was eliminated by subsequent congressional action.

Ida never seemed to have much regard for labels. "I don't call myself a wheat queen or any other kind of a queen, remember that," she said. "The folks around here hitched that nickname onto me. . . . I know I am no queen, but just a hard-working old Mrs. Farmer, doing my best to help feed this old world, and getting fairly well paid for it."[19]

10

Laura Alderman

"Queen of Orchardists"

"WHAT I PARTICULARLY DESIRE AT THIS TIME IS TO IMPRESS UPON your minds this one fact, that to woman, and not to man, we South Dakotans are indebted for the 'corner stone' of South Dakota horticulture," a writer in the *First Annual Report of the South Dakota State Horticultural Society* stated in 1904. "It was she, not he, that demonstrated to the world that apples of a size, beauty and flavor could be successfully grown in South Dakota that would put to blush any grown in the famous fruit states of Michigan or Missouri."[1] The writer was referring to Laura Alderman of Alderman Fruit Farm, located near Hurley, South Dakota. Established in 1879 by Laura and her husband, Olynthus, the business had been jokingly known as "Alderman's Folly" in the early years, when no one believed fruit could be successfully grown in South Dakota.[2] But in 1901, when Laura sold the renowned orchard for $12,000 and retired to sunny California, no one was calling it a folly. Identified as the largest orchard in South Dakota by the state's chief pomologist, Laura's eight thousand apple trees spread over 150 acres yielded eight thousand to ten thousand bushels of fruit each year.

For twenty-two years, Laura, a "brisk, cheery, and intelligent talker" by one account, had poured all her resources into the family business, transforming the prairie sod to rows and rows of Duchess, Wealthy, Whitney, and Tetofski apple trees.[3] Laura became the primary manager of the orchard as Olynthus's mental health declined and the pair eventually divorced. "Our orchard was not so much planned as developed," she said about the early years. "In the pioneer days of Dakota we sold a large quantity of nursery stock. Many people who ordered trees were unable to pay for them, and the trees were left on our hands." So the resourceful Aldermans planted the trees and observed which varieties adapted well to the Dakota climate. She explained, "[W]e became convinced that the outlook justified the experiment of an extensive commercial orchard. Our present orchard is the result."[4]

Laura Alderman. Saint Paul Globe, *January 5, 1901.*

The Aldermans took their produce to the local fairs to introduce neighbors to their new endeavor. In late September 1885, they attended the first annual Territorial Fair in Huron, where they showcased their canned fruits and jellies, and their Wealthy apples took first premium. The local paper proclaimed, "[T]he exhibit demonstrates beyond all question that fruit can be raised in Dakota."[5] At the 1886 fair, the Aldermans' fruits again won recognition as well as a little cash for the family—$97, including $30 for "best collection of fruit grown in Dakota or Minnesota."[6] And at the 1887 fair in Mitchell, where fairgoers were awed by a 24½-pound cabbage, 169-pound pumpkin, and an unbelievable 120-pound squash, the Aldermans "made a grand display of apples, crabs, grapes, plums."[7]

In 1896, Laura sat down for an interview with the Sioux Falls *Argus-Leader* newspaper, which identified her as the manager and owner of the orchard. She reported that the business had produced four thousand bushels that sold for an average price of sixty cents per bushel that year. Some had even brought as much as a dollar a bushel. One hundred acres of the ranch were covered in a "solid block" of rows of apple trees at right angles with each other. Laura explained that workers took great care in training branches to grow close to the ground so that high winds would not sway the trees and loosen the roots. The practice also allowed the low limbs to shade the body of the tree and prevent sun scalding and helped retain moisture in the soil around the trees. Laura said she had never needed to invest a great deal in costly machinery, as planting and harvesting simply required reliable workers. In the spring, tent caterpillars required the attention of a man for about a month as he fought to eradicate the pests. All he needed to do his job was a stepladder and a "pair of good buckskin gloves" to strip off the tentlike nests from the branches.[8]

Not surprisingly, Alderman Fruit Farm experienced off years when their output suffered—1897 was one of those, when only 1,500 bushels were sold. But over the years, the Aldermans had also invested in other fruits. So in 1897, the slow apple production was offset by the sale of fifteen bushels of cherries and four thousand quarts of strawberries. Additionally, they raised plums, pears, cherries, and apricots. "[T]he strawberry garden, covering five acres, with its irrigating plant insuring a constant water supply, has remained an important factor of our business," Laura explained. And by 1898, apple production had rebounded with a banner year of eight thousand bushels. The Aldermans were credited with providing a "distinct service to the state" by encouraging South Dakotans to purchase fruit in the state rather than in such states as Michigan and Iowa. Laura, who had lived for a time in Iowa, had this to say: "I like Dakota better than Iowa and think it is better for farming and fruit raising."[9]

As the reputation of Alderman Fruit Farm grew, the business and its owner became known outside South Dakota. Publications across the country published articles about the "pioneer woman apple grower" and the "Woman Orchardist."[10] *Frank Leslie's Weekly*, a national publication in New York City, ran a short article about the Aldermans' orchard located "[o]ut in a country of large things" and offering the "finest fruit that the latitude affords," with a photo of Laura, who showed "pluck and energy" as she went about her duties each day.[11] Her fame also made her a target of "people seeking to make matches by correspondence" and matrimonial agencies wanting her to enroll—as she would make a "splendid matrimonial prize."[12] Laura was mostly amused by all the attention. And when a reporter from the *New York Tribune* inquired about the suitability of her work for women, she responded, "I should say that while it does not seem particularly fitted to them there is no valid reason why they should not engage in it. The line of demarcation between men's and women's work, you know, is growing more shadowy with the receding years. Success in business ventures is not a 'question of beards,' but of business capacity."[13]

Laura preferred to hire women and children from nearby towns to pick her crop at harvest time. Smaller kids climbed the trees, while older ones used stepladders to reach lower branches. Women oversaw the operation and emptied the sacks into the barrels, watching for second-class or bruised fruit. Each picker received a number on a piece of paper at the beginning of the work. The number was placed on each package filled by a picker, and at the end of each day, the worker was paid according to the number of bushels filled. Pay ranged from two to five cents per bushel. During harvest, Laura had as many as forty pickers.

"Our select stock is shipped to retail dealers in cities and villages north and west of us," Laura said. "They are sent directly from the farm or in car lots to some central point, where they are redistributed."[14]

In 1901, with bushels totaling close to ten thousand, the Alderman Fruit Farm had its best year ever and the largest crop of apples ever produced in the region. While attending the Minnesota Horticultural Society meeting in early January, Laura, in an interview with the *Minneapolis Journal*, hinted at things to come. "There are times when the handling of a crop of 8,000 or 10,000 bushels of apples in August and September taxes our resource to the utmost," she said.[15] She further explained, "I have about all I can manage myself, and I don't care to have more than I can handle directly."[16] A month later, it was announced that Laura had sold the Alderman Fruit Farm.

This "queen of orchardists" was fondly recognized by the South Dakota State Horticultural Society a few years later: "[N]either drought, grasshoppers, hard times, or anything else swerved her from her purpose. She never lost faith in the country, the soil, the climate, or herself. She was determined to succeed and she did succeed, and today South Dakota is proud of her and her work."[17]

PART V

COWGIRLS

"Any bright morning in the latter part of May I am out of bed at four o'clock; next after I have dressed and combed my hair, I start a fire in the kitchen stove, and while the stove is getting hot I go to my flower garden and gather a choice, half-blown rose and a spray of bride's wreath, and arrange them in my hair, and sweep the floors and then cook breakfast. While the other members of the family are eating breakfast I strain away the morning's milk and fill my husband's dinner pail, for he will go to work on our other farm for the day."[1]

11

Marion Carterett Reese

Cowgirl, Stagecoach Driver, and Artist

IT WAS SAID THAT MARION CARTERETT REESE NEVER KNEW THE MEAN-
ing of fear, "never recognized the existence of danger," and never considered the "possibility of failure."[1] It was those characteristics that lured
her into a lifetime fascination for wild horses and a stint as a champion
bronco buster around the rodeo circuits in Nevada, Wyoming, and Utah
and in the legendary Pendleton Round-Up in Oregon, first held in 1910
with an attendance of seven thousand.

Born in 1892 to western rancher parents, Marion learned to ride
before she walked—tucked snugly in the saddle with her dad—and rode
solo by the time she was a toddler. After the deaths of her parents, she
went to live on her uncle's ranch in Montana, where her love of horses
flourished. But when a cousin detected an artistic spark in Marion as a
teenager, he generously offered to send her off to art school in Boston.
She could never shake her homesickness for the horses back on the ranch,
though, and left before completing her course of study. "My cousin never
forgave me for that. Ever since then, my horses have been both my success
·and my undoing," Marion said years later.[2]

After leaving art school, Marion persistently pursued work that
allowed her to remain close to the horses she loved. She taught riding
lessons at a livery in Boise, Idaho, for a while and in 1911 taught school
at the Western Shoshone Indian Reservation in Nevada while delivering mail by horseback in the reservation. For a couple years, she drove
a stagecoach in Montana and Idaho. "That job was an interesting one,"

Marion reminisced about her nontraditional work choices. Sometimes passengers were taken aback when they realized their driver was a female, but Marion liked to tell the story about the time she filled in for a male driver who had gotten drunk at one of the stops between Red Creek, Montana, and Salmon City, Idaho. His passengers were certainly rattled by his dangerous and erratic driving, so when a substitute was found to complete the trip, they breathed a collective sigh of relief—until they got a closer look at the substitute. "When they saw me, a woman driver, take over, it did not help much even though they were grateful to know I was thoroughly sober," Marion recalled.[3]

Marion soon realized she had her own set of problems as she navigated the peaks and winding mountain roads—with no brakes! "The only possible way I could keep the heavy coach from running into the horses down those steep grades and frightening them into a runaway, was to whip them and keep them going at top speed," she said. And, thanks to Marion's driving skills and command of the horses, the stage safely reached its destination with no mishaps. She mused, "I never discovered exactly what my passengers thought, but I am quite sure those city ladies were frightened almost to death. But then so was I."[4]

However, fear was not in Marion's vocabulary when she took to the rodeo circuit in 1912. She joined a growing number of intrepid women who rode, roped, and wrangled and wowed audiences throughout the West. From Los Angeles and Cheyenne to Pendleton and Calgary, Canada, the ladies competed for attention and prize money. Marion and her sisterhood of athletes competed in relay and lassoing contests, bucking bronco and bucking mule competitions, steer wrestling and roping, and bull riding. Marion shared the spotlight with Fannie Sperry Steele, crowned World Champion bronc rider in 1912 and 1913, who, with her rodeo-clown husband, spent her honeymoon on the rodeo tour. Tillie Baldwin, an immigrant from Norway and a former hairdresser, worked as a trick rider, bronc rider, and steer wrestler. Prairie Rose Henderson, like Marion, grew up riding and enchanted the crowd at the second annual Los Angeles Rodeo in 1913. Known for her outstanding bronc riding, she also was memorable for her over-the-top costumes—of course the typical cowgirl boots, but there was nothing typical about her bloomers topped off with sequins and ostrich feathers.

Cowgirls at the Pendleton Round-Up in 1911. *M. B. Marcell, copyright claimant, M. B. Marcell, photographer. "Cow Girls" at the Pendleton "Round-Up." Pendleton, Oregon, United States, 1911. loc.gov/item/2007663536/.*

Marion joined the ranks of this dauntless cavalcade of athletes entertaining crowds of thousands across the West. While the venues changed and the spectacles went by a variety of names—*rodeo, roundup, stampede, frontier days*—the spectators came to expect a raucous, rambunctious celebration of impressive trick riding, amazing stunts, and dusty tumbles mingled with the "whoop of a hundred cowboys," all "punctuated by the indignant snorts" of bucking broncos and raging bulls.[5]

Plans were under way in Elko, Nevada, in the summer of 1914 to provide spectators of the third annual rodeo with an experience like none other. Management was spending $1,000 to ensure the grounds and track would be in first-class condition, preparations were in the works for a free barbeque, and prize monies of $1,500 ($500 each day) were ready to award. And the wildest horses possible were being fed grain and exercised daily to "give them good wind and staying powers."[6] The crowds that gathered on September 7, 8, and 9 were not disappointed. The best riders from the circuit were brought into Elko to try to conquer the worst horses on the range. Spectators were treated to "nerve-terrifying memories of the days when breaking the wind of a bucking broncho was a before breakfast pastime."[7] The crowds got a little boisterous as they rushed into the grandstand to watch the wild horse race—causing a prominent rancher, William Hunter, to suffer multiple bruises and a couple of broken ribs—but overall, the three-day festivities were considered a giant success. It was here that Marion "won her spurs" competing with rodeo performers

at the PENDLETON "ROUND UP" 1911

from eight states to win the women's riding championship.[8] Elko's *Weekly Independent* claimed she had displayed "considerable skill" and provided "splendid exhibitions of riding."[9]

By this time, Marion had earned a reputation as being "skilled with the reins as well as in the saddle." Her stagecoach-driving days over mountain roads had honed her skills at handling teams, and she was well known as a woman who could skillfully maneuver a team of fourteen horses by the subtle touch of her reins or the command of her voice—the "master degree in horsemanship." She was recognized as an able rider of some of the most vicious outlaw horses (the wildest, toughest, meanest, untamable horses to be found)—according to one account, the "only woman in the United States" who had succeeded in riding "at least three" outlaw horses that had been "responsible for the deaths of skilled men riders." But Marion's riding days had taken a toll on her body as those horses, "trying in vain to throw her," had fallen on top of her.[10] "I was hurt pretty badly inside on some of those falls," she said. "Finally the doctors told me they wouldn't be responsible for my life if I kept riding."[11]

Marion decided to retire from her career as a performing cowgirl. She had earned a reputation as a skilled athlete and an admirable opponent— "idolized by her associates."[12] But she knew when it was time to hang up her spurs.

Her days at the "riproaring, dust whirling, blood spilling exhibitions" of the rodeo circuit behind, she applied for—and made news by winning over several male candidates—the position of postmistress of Deeth, Nevada.[13] "It used to be a railroad station named Death," Marion explained some years later as she spoke about the appointment. "Somebody thought

Marion Carterett Reese. *The* Weekly Independent, *Independent Publications, Incorporated, Vol. 83, 1915.*

Deeth would be less gruesome."[14]

She held the job for only a few months and married a fellow, adopting his last name and thereby becoming Marion Reese. Although the marriage didn't last, she and her husband operated a successful trucking business in Idaho, and she became quite adept at driving a Diamond T truck and a Model T truck. "If you've never

ELKO RODEO
Bucking Horses Wanted
We will give $10.00 in cash to the owners of outlaw horses for every time one of our riders is thrown at the
BIG RODEO IN ELKO
September 7, 8 and 9, 1914
Feed bills while here at our expense. Horses bought at end of Rodeo if they're mean enough and can buck enough
Bring in your bucking horses and get a little easy money
G. S. GARCIA

Advertisement in Nevada newspaper shortly before rodeo. Daily Independent, *Elko, Nevada, August 24, 1914.*

driven a Model T truck 250 miles a day over primitive roads, you can have no idea of how I felt," she said in a 1948 interview.[15] After her marriage ended, Marion moved to Arizona with her deaf dog, Smoky, and took up prospecting. She spent her days panning and testing her discoveries for lucrative finds. And she revived her artistic endeavors, turning some of her gems and minerals into such artistic objects as ashtrays and vases that she sold at a Prescott gift shop. And she turned to painting pictures of stagecoaches and horses that looked as though they "were walking off across the plains."[16] Although she had offers from horse owners seeking a skilled horse trainer, she turned them down. "It is terribly tempting and I would love to do it," she said. "But I no longer can give them the care and attention they deserve and must have."[17]

Marion had no regrets about the path her life took after she left art school as a teen. "I don't think I could change any of my life. It has been rich in adventure. If I can't ride any longer, I have many pleasant memories which I enjoy re-creating with a paint brush," she said.[18]

Ollie Osborn

Holding Her Own with the Best of 'Em

EVERY SATURDAY, AS MARY ELLEN OSBORN SET OUT FOR TOWN FROM the family ranch near Union, Oregon, in the early 1900s to do her weekly shopping, she expected her children to keep busy with practical chores. But the kids had other ideas about how to fill those unsupervised hours. Forgetting that their mother had admonished to stay away from the horses, Ollie and her siblings found it a perfect time to stage a family rodeo featuring horse racing and bronc breaking. "Let 'er buck," Ollie's brothers shouted as she mounted a barely broke horse.[1] Those illicit adventures by the disobedient Osborn kids planted the seeds for Ollie to eventually become a celebrity cowgirl riding the rodeo circuit in Wild West shows across the country until her retirement in 1932.

By the time Ollie was a teenager, she was entering and winning horse relay races and bucking competitions at local and regional roundups and stock shows. While the relay races were mostly about speed, those horses could also present a challenge. "They'd outrun anything in the world when they got to running, but they take time out to buck too," Ollie said. She rode in the famed Pendleton Round-Up in Oregon in 1913 as part of the cowgirls' relay team that captured second place for "championship of the world."[2] Later that same month, at Walla Walla Frontier Days in Washington, Ollie took third in the girls' relay, a three-day event where riders rode two miles a day, changing horses every half mile. In 1914, back at Pendleton, where the cowgirls' relay race "brought the crowd to its feet" and the track was wet from an early-morning rain, Ollie took a hard-fought fourth place.[3] And she rode again in the sixth annual Pendleton event in 1915, where the "world's most reckless" cowgirls and -boys who were "willing to risk life and limb for a chance to win a little money and a great deal of acclaim from an admiring multitude" competed while riding the "greatest assemblage of equine deviltry ever assembled in one corral."[4] And again in 1916, Ollie competed at Pendleton, this time taking third place in the horse-bucking contest. Later that month, at the Union Stock Show in Union, Oregon, she won thirty-five dollars in the three-day women's relay race and wowed the hometown crowd with her performances in the women's bucking-horse exhibition and in the men's bucking-bull contest. Back at Pendleton in 1918, Ollie won second place in the ladies' bucking contest.

Ollie had proven herself in all those hair-raising competitions, and her jaw-dropping stunts had been noticed by well-known Wild West show producers, as well as a movie producer. Edmund, better known as "Hoot," Gibson begged her to come to Hollywood and go into the moving-picture business. "I can get you in like nobody's business," he said. But she refused. "I wanted to travel," Ollie said years later. And she believed a life in pictures would be too confining—"corralled in one spot," as she saw it—for a young woman who wanted to move about. "I didn't want to sit," she said.[5] When Charles Irwin of Irwin Brothers Wild West Shows offered Ollie a contract for exhibition riding, she jumped at the chance to earn a living doing what she loved and to travel the country from coast to coast. It was the beginning of a thrilling career for Ollie.

All through the 1920s, Ollie was a member of the elite group of women rodeo performers who executed bold stunts, balancing precariously on the backs of wild horses and clinging with all their might to the tops of bucking horses and snorting bulls. At times, they competed with men riders, showing the world that women were just as rugged and competent as the men. Everyone in the rodeo world knew a rider enjoyed a certain advantage when atop a bucking horse with hobbled stirrups—that is, stirrups securely tied under the horse's belly. Some women riders preferred using the hobbled stirrups, but Ollie proudly favored "riding slick" on unhobbled broncs. "It's a harder way of riding," she said.[6]

Pendleton Round-Up in 1913. *F. W. Sheelor, copyright claimant. The Round-Up, Pendleton, Oregon. Pendleton, Oregon, United States, ca. 1913. loc.gov/item/2007663795/.*

Rodeogoers were often intrigued with the female performers' clothes. Ollie wore leather riding skirts when bouncing about on her rearing broncs in the early days of her career, but later she took to wearing pants. She wasn't a fan of the colored bloomers she and the other women wore in the relay races, and they never wore expensive shirts during the races because "you take a chance getting them tore off you." And the investment the women had in their clothes, boots, and equipment could become quite costly. Just like the men, Ollie and other women earned salaries for their work in the shows, but simply because they were males, the men usually were paid more than the women. Some people justified the pay discrepancy by claiming the women were given special treatment—such as tamer horses to ride. But Ollie insisted it wasn't the case: "[W]e hollered for the men's bucking horses, we got them. We rode the same the men rode and many shows I rode the same horses the men rode, many shows."[7]

From the start, Mr. Irwin expected the best from his performers—male or female. "I'll have you all killed off before we get to New York, or I'll make top riders out of you," he joked. And did he make top riders out of them as promised? "Oh, yeah!" according to Ollie. And she proved it in a New York City show, where she stubbornly stayed on an especially big horse that was a favorite of men riders—and she won first place. "I'm

telling you, talk about a bucking horse, he was a bucking horse," Ollie said. "[H]e used his hips like a bull bucks."[8]

A popular rodeo event with fans was steer wrestling, or bulldogging. Men and women performers took part in the sport, and it required a certain toughness and dexterity. "[Y]ou walk your horse, you grab their [the steer's] horns, twist their head over and if you're stout enough, down they came," Ollie said. It wasn't Ollie's favorite; she tried it once in a Portland show with a friend but never again. She recalled, "We said after that, they can have the dog, we don't want it. . . . [W]e thought once was enough."[9]

Ollie was proud that she made enough money to support herself over the years. As a young competitor in her teen years, her pay varied. Sometimes her reward was a prize, such as a saddle. Other times, payment for winning races or bucking contests was as much as $300 or $400. During her Irwin Show days, her contract provided her $60 a month plus room and board and half of her arena earnings, equaling about $100 per month.[10] The performers pooled their resources as they traveled to shows. They'd get a car and squeeze five or six in to share expenses. "[W]e had lots and lots of fun in our travels," Ollie said. When people questioned the wisdom in sharing such close quarters with the cowboys, who by some accounts were a rowdy bunch, Ollie became defensive. "[Y]ou're more safe with an ol' tough cowboy than some of your city boys any day in the week," she said.[11]

Ollie Osborn, 1982 Cowgirl Honoree—Oregon. *National Cowgirl Museum and Hall of Fame, Fort Worth, Texas.*

Ollie was realistic about life as a rodeo performer. "Yes, it's rough and tiresome. . . . [Y]ou've got to be pretty strong to stay with it . . . but when you are riding every day, it's the best muscle builder there is . . . horseback riding," she said.[12] Ollie recalled one especially memorable little horse named Clearwater: "[H]e was a beautiful thing and he had some tricky ways about him. He'd buck so long and he'd stand on his hind feet till he'd scare the life outta ya." She also was modest: "Well, don't like to brag on myself but think I hold my own with the best of 'um."[13]

PART VI

HOMESTEADERS

"I suppose it is impossible for a woman to do her best at everything which she would like to do, but I really would like to. I almost cut sleep out of my routine in trying to keep up all the rows which I have started in on; in the short winter days I must get the cooking and house straightening done in addition to looking after stock and poultry, and make a garment occasionally, and wash and iron the clothes; all the other work is done after night by lamp light, and when the work for the day is over, or at least the most pressing part of it, and the family are all asleep and no one to forbid it, I spend a few hours writing or reading."[1]

Anna Porter and Maud Sterling

"Girls on the Mountain"

"Afraid-of-a-mouse kind" of women should not consider life as a homesteader, according to Anna Porter.[1] And she knew something about homesteading, as she had spent five years on a claim she named Wildwood a few miles outside Spokane in Washington State. Plenty of single women like Anna had filed claims for lands that had been made available through the Homestead Act of 1862 and subsequent federal legislation in 1873, 1877, and 1909.[2] How many of those were "afraid-of-a-mouse" kind of homesteaders is unknown, but their experiences were widely recounted in popular magazines at the time. And the *Spokesman-Review* newspaper in Spokane featured Anna and her neighbor, Maud Sterling, in a splashy spread in the women's section of the July 9, 1911, Sunday edition.

After five years of clearing, planting, and building, the "girls on the mountain," as the locals called the two women, had "proved up" their claim, gaining title to 160 acres each. It hadn't come easily, and they had entertaining stories to tell.[3] Anna had already built her little cabin on Wildwood when Maud set up her abode, naming it Echo. She had strategically chosen the site for her cabin by climbing a tree and surveying her property and ultimately selected a spot that would afford a dynamic view of Liberty Lake. Building and furnishing their homes was an ordeal. They had all the timber they could wish for, and they had brought axes, so felling trees was a regular pastime. But they did not have access to a saw-mill, so maneuvering logs and fashioning them into furniture and housing

Anna and Maud featured in the *Spokesman-Review*, July 9, 1911. Spokesman-Review *in Newspapers.com.*

material was challenging. They estimated that over the five years, they had cleared about fifteen acres of timber between the two homesteads.

Anna and Maud told the *Spokesman-Review* reporter about the time fires threatened their cabins. There had been talk among the neighbors that wildfires were approaching, and when they spotted smoke and wildlife, including bears, moving at a rather rapid pace in one direction, the two friends knew they were in danger. The women hunkered down in Maud's cabin near the water source and worked throughout the night to save the cabin. Lugging pails of water from the stream and stamping out little fires as fast as possible, the two saved the cabin from ruin. In the morning, expecting to find Anna's cabin a charred mess, they were surprised to discover the house intact, thanks to the winds shifting just enough to spare the Wildwood structure. Even the delicate flowers Anna had planted around the house were spared.

Men did participate in Anna and Maud's homesteading experience. Both Maud's and Anna's dads came to visit, and Maud's brother had helped construct her cabin. Anna's little nephew Walter spent the entire spring of 1912 on Wildwood. But it was Maud's "gentle, kind, wagtail" male dog, Bowser, who contributed the most loyal support to the homestead endeavor.[4] According to the *Spokesman-Review*, Bowser had been instrumental in helping Maud select her cabin site back when she first established her homestead.

And this "indefatigable chaser of game" was a marvel at stalking pheasants and grouse. Pheasants seemed to be especially frightened by the mighty Bowser. It was common practice for him to tree a bird, keeping the feathery creature paralyzed with fear, while he waited for his mistress to respond to his frantic barks. "My gun maybe will kick or I have to shoot three times before I do anything but knock his feathers off," Maud said. "But it isn't any kind of hunting sport when the dog scares him into being a target."[5]

The intrepid Bowser feared nothing, it seemed. One day, Maud set out to act on Bowser's summons, crawling under logs and brush to reach the dog circling the tree where the creature—a pheasant Maud presumed—lurked overhead. Just as Maud raised her .22 rifle to the treetop, she saw an "awful furry animal face" observing her every move. Bowser had treed a mighty cougar, who "would look at me contemplatively . . . perhaps to see whether or not I would make good eating," she said. "I was too scared to shoot." Maud backed out of her perch and ran back to the cabin, seeking a helpful hand from Anna, and the two hurried back to the spot where Bowser continued his watch. Anna and Maud positioned themselves on opposite sides of the tree as they discussed how to proceed. Although Anna wanted to take a shot, they questioned the wisdom of this, as they feared for Bowser's life. As Maud described the location of the beast for Anna, she responded, "Yes, I can see his whole body and his tail." Maud was puzzled by that reply, thinking it impossible for her friend to see the animal from her position. "Why no you can't from that point," Maud said. "Yes, but I do," Anna insisted.[6] And as Maud moved to stand beside her friend, the two realized Bowser had cornered *two* fearsome cougars. In the end, the women spared the cougars' lives.

Anna and Maud soon learned that homesteading could be an expensive enterprise. Although homesteaders acquired the land as their own after fulfilling the requirements to live on the premises for a specified period of time (three to five years) and make improvements, they incurred expenses, too. Those could become quite significant. Initially, there was a filing fee with the government—as high as $25—and a surveyor's fee up to $100.[7] Although Anna and Maud had gardens, made mattresses from pine branches and furniture from simple logs, they had other expenses, such as tools and cooking supplies. And because their expenses "had a way of piling up to be paid," they spent part of the year working off their claims.[8] They both got jobs at fruit farms, thinning apples. And as was often the case with women, their clothing was a topic of interest. The *Spokesman-Review* reported that the two "girls on the mountain" laughed at women who worked out of doors in "trailing skirts." Anna and Maud chose to wear the "breeches, boots and shirts of their backwoods home."[9]

Although the newspaper declared Anna and Maud looked "boyish and picturesque," the two were less concerned with their looks than they were with simply surviving and succeeding in making the homesteads their own. Armed with rifles and dressed in "rough and ready costumes," Anna and Maud became accustomed to hiking nine miles for the nearest supply source, six miles to a post office, and more than two miles to the nearest neighbor. But as the *Spokesman-Review* reported, the girls on the mountain were "two determined women" who proved up their homestead claims as well as their courage.[10] And they had proved they were not the "afraid-of-a-mouse" kind of women.

Nannita Daisey

"Leaping into History"

ON THE EVENING OF FEBRUARY 1, 1884, THE STATEHOUSE IN FRANK-fort, Kentucky, erupted into chaos as the all-male body of lawmakers "turned into a howling, surging sea of strife" while hundreds of feminine voices reigned down from the gallery: "Let 'em fight"; "Put 'em out"; "Give it to him." The position of state librarian, which the legislators were tasked with selecting, was at stake, and when two lawmakers fell into a pushing match, fellow legislators stepped in to pull the two apart. One, his "disordered hair and face red with rage," struggled to free himself from their grasps. Six candidates for the job had been introduced by the lawmakers, and as roll call votes commenced, lawmakers stood on top of their desks, "contending wildly" and "gesticulating frantically," as a "current of anger" swept through the chambers "like a wave of fire" and the spectators in the galleries "arose as a unit and swelled the frenzied furor."[1] By the time Assistant Chief of Police Percy Smith and one of his detectives arrived to help restore order, the men were already well into multiple roll call votes, as one candidate after another lost out to the voting.

Finally, only one candidate remained after six votes—Virginia Hanson, a widow of a Confederate officer. She had spent the years after the war raising funds for disabled confederate soldiers and orphans' homes. The two-year librarian's position paid $1,000 per year, and it was a coveted job typically reserved for women. One of the candidates was a woman named Nannita Daisey, a "lady who had by her own efforts educated and supported herself" and whose "triumphs were greater than any won on a field of battle," according to the state lawmaker who had nominated her. Although she failed to win the position for the second time, having lost out in 1881 also, Nannita "took her defeat with exceeding good grace."[2]

Orphaned at a young age, Nannita had gone to live at an orphanage in St. Louis, Missouri. Armed with an education from the nuns who ran the orphanage, by 1880, she was teaching in Jeffersontown, a town about ten miles from Louisville, Kentucky.[3] The school, located in "delightful surroundings" just outside the city, served about seventy students, all of whom were "devotedly attached" to Nannita, who had the "temperament, tact and talent of the successful teacher" and "whose soul is filled to overflowing with a love for the work."[4] She had moved to a job at the First-Ward public school in Louisville for the 1883–1884 school year, teaching fourth grade. Her students were fond of her there, too, presenting her with a "beautiful plush photograph album" inscribed "To Miss Nannetta [*sic*] R. H. Daisey, from her class of 1883–'84" at the close of the school term.[5] Despite the students' enthusiasm for their teacher, one news report indicated she left the Louisville school when she "quarreled with the trustees."[6]

But she had built a reputation as a respected educator and speaker over the years; she gave a teaching demonstration in mental arithmetic at a county teachers' institute in 1880 and spoke to the state General Assembly in 1881 about education reform. According to a report in the *Owensboro Messenger*, she "acquitted herself splendidly and bravely" as she made "many sensible and valuable suggestions" in her address to the lawmakers.[7] Outside her education work, Nannita found time to participate in the local branch of the Irish National League, where she also "showed her elocutionary powers" at the monthly meetings.[8] In addition to her teaching and speaking activities, she yearned to be a journalist and eventually found her way into work as a reporter for several newspapers. It was during one of her reporting assignments that Nannita became the object of a story herself.

On April 22, 1889, the US government opened to non-Indian settlers the territory known as the Unassigned Lands in the Territory of Oklahoma.[9] Speculators and ordinary citizens were eager to rush in and claim 160-acre tracts. It was a newsworthy event covered by many newspapers,

Oklahoma Land Rush in April 1889 mural by John Steuart Curry. *Library of Congress Prints and Photographs Division, Washington, D.C. 20540 LC-DIG-highsm-24969. Photographs in the Carol M. Highsmith Archive.*

including the *Dallas Morning News*, which sent Nannita to cover the story.[10] And while she was eager to report on the land grab, Nannita also saw an opportunity to claim a tract for herself. Having scouted the area beforehand, she picked a spot she intended to claim. On the day of the opening, she rode a train that brought news reporters into the area. "I stood in with the engineer," she said. "When I got in sight of my claim I gave the engineer a signal. He began to slow up." She continued, "When I got even with my claim I gave a jump while the train was in motion. As the train went by I planted my stakes, threw my cloak over one, then fell on my knees and discharged my revolver in the air exclaiming, 'This I salute the Kentucky Daisey's claim!'"[11]

This version of Nannita's efforts to obtain a piece of land subsequently was altered by countless reports at the time and became part of local lore. According to the somewhat more sensational story, Nannita perched herself precariously on the cowcatcher of the train engine and after jumping off at the location of her desired claim sank to her knees, fired two revolvers in the air, ripped her petticoat from under her skirts, and attached it to a nearby bush to validate her claim. Regardless of which account people wanted to believe, Nannita did stake her claim and settled into the nearby community.

She built a small cabin on her land and started a school in Guthrie, Oklahoma. When someone suggested she run for mayor, she said, "I believe I'll make the race."[12] But that one person seemed to be the only one who would commit to her candidacy, so Nannita abandoned the idea.

But her thirst for land had not waned, and when the federal government opened another area to Anglo settlement, Nannita was ready to acquire her share. In 1891, land grabbers prepared to claim lots in the area that would become Chandler, Oklahoma. As one newspaper described it, "Where a week ago the Iowa and Sac and Fox Indians roamed," thousands of Anglo settlers "have taken up the work of a civilized and settled country."[13]

By now, Nannita had become a bit of a national celebrity, with newspapers across the country carrying articles about "Kentucky Daisey."[14] And her

The Oklahoma home of Nannita Daisey years after she lived in it had fallen into disrepair and was ultimately demolished. *University of Central Oklahoma, Chambers Library, Archives/Special Collections, Edmond, Oklahoma.*

role in the latest land-rush event was captured by papers. At exactly twelve noon on September 22, a "volley of musketry" was released, and the hordes rushed in to claim town lots. It was reported that Nannita, "riding a spirited horse with a man's saddle," was among them and had been thrown from her mount, hitting her head on a large rock and causing her death.[15] It turned out the report of her death was inaccurate, and Nannita recovered from the fall and claimed her lot in Chandler.

Even the *New York Times* reported on the exploits of the "irrepressible Annetta Daisy [*sic*]" in 1892.[16] This time, Nannita was helping a band of single women who, coming from six states, had formed in Kansas City and hoped to claim lands in Oklahoma, as Nannita had back in 1889. Her previous experience as a land rusher and homesteader prepared her for this job as a consultant of sorts. Under the leadership and guidance of Nannita, the women had been secretly camping out for a week in a secluded gulch within the borders of the soon-to-be-available lands in a position to make the run in a group as soon as the signal was given. The *Times* was discreet in its reporting to protect the location of the band, but it was clear the women were determined. Armed with rifles, revolvers, and horses, the group were intent on eluding authorities, who would rut them out if detected. Maintaining military-like discipline, the women guarded their lair day and night with their guns, and Nannita set out under the cover of darkness to get supplies from the nearest town. However, as she rode back to the secret hideout, two cavalrymen who happened to be scouting for sooners intercepted Nannita and prevented her from reaching the women with their supplies. The fate of the band of women and their attempts at owning land are unclear.

Nannita's reputation as a pioneer homesteader was legendary, and typically, she was referred to in glowing terms: "restless and daring as a cowboy, warm hearted, true to her friends."[17] She ended her days in Chicago, where she died in 1903. The subsequent news articles about her passing usually included such descriptors as "Kentucky Daisy," "first feminine homesteader," and "persistent," as well as recalled the more flamboyant petticoat version of her Oklahoma homesteading claim.[18] Years after her death, people continued to remember her as an intriguing figure from Kentucky's and Oklahoma's pasts.

In 1910, she was prominent in a local news article about the role of women homesteaders in the state's development—women who answered a "call of the wild." In 1927, the *Los Angeles Times* reported that Alma Carson, a teacher from Guthrie, Oklahoma, and niece of Kit Carson, was advocating for the building of a monument dedicated to the women homesteaders of the state, including Nannita, who had been "occupying a front seat in Oklahoma's march of progress."[19] In 2007, the town of Edmond, Oklahoma, unveiled a sculpture honoring Nannita Daisey and her irrepressible spirit as a homesteader in the rough-and-tumble days of Oklahoma's past. It is titled *Leaping into History*.[20]

Glenna Lynch

From Chicago Dressmaker to Western Landowner

"We want workers, not idlers. Women who would not rather follow a plow than work all day at a sewing machine will not do."[1]

GLENNA LYNCH TRIED TO BE AS DIRECT AS POSSIBLE WHEN DESCRIBING the type of adventurous women she sought for the development of a ranch near Wendell, Idaho, in 1908. The twenty-year-old Chicago seamstress had spearheaded the effort to organize a group to leave their factory jobs in the city for a farming venture out West. She had succeeded in enticing Adelaide Jackson, Marie Miller, Laura Hunt, Helen Miller, and Maud Lynch to form the Idaho Guild and contribute parts of their wages to the purchase of 160 acres of land. The women had met through their association with the Artcraft Institute Guild, a "combined school and club for the promotion of practical art and industrial education" for women founded by T.

Newspaper advertisement targeting settlers to Idaho. Idaho Statesman *(Boise, Idaho)*, *Sept. 24, 1909.*

Vernette Morse in 1900 that promised to "meet the diversified demands and conditions of everyday life."[2] Glenna affirmed her commitment to the land-buying enterprise when a Chicago reporter questioned her: "Shall I plow? I most certainly will. I have been long enough slaving away sewing in this city. Any kind of farm work will suit me all right."[3]

By the summer of 1909, the members of the Idaho Guild had made their last installment payment for the land purchase. Their tract was situated in an area supported by the Twin Falls Irrigation Project, which had been developed through the Carey Act, passed by Congress in 1894, which made it possible to transform desertlike land into irrigated farmland. Private companies built infrastructure such as canals, and US citizens at least twenty-one years old, including unmarried women, could apply for a purchase of land. With a one-dollar entry fee and one-half of the purchase price of the land (fifty cents per acre), an adventurous, hardworking individual could acquire 160 acres of land.[4] Buyers were required to fulfill certain terms, such as constructing ditches to nearby canals, cultivating and irrigating a portion of the land, building a habitable dwelling, and paying the second half of the purchase price. In addition, they were

Workers at camp at head of canal, Milner Dam & Main Canal: Twin Falls Canal Company, on Snake River, 11 miles west of Burley, Idaho, Twin Falls, Idaho. *Library of Congress Prints and Photographs Division, Washington, D.C. HAER ID,27-TWIF.V,1—161.*

required to pay for water rights. Glenna was chosen to travel to Idaho to explore the possibilities for the best use of the Idaho Guild's investment.

As the time for her departure drew near, Glenna expressed her enthusiasm for the project: "Oh, I have been told about the miles and miles of sage brush, with no sign of life except jackrabbits, but I am not afraid of the prospect—nor the jackrabbits either." She added, "We came to the conclusion a year ago that the irrigated farms of the west offered a field of work for women, and our beliefs have not been shaken. I expect to find out whether it is really practical for women to go west and personally take charge of operations, and, if I find it is—as I am confident I shall—most of us are ready to move."[5] In August 1909, her friends and business partners celebrated her departure with a gathering and gifted her a silver "toilet set," a mirror, brushes, and other dressing-table paraphernalia for her morning grooming. Their thoughtfulness was greatly appreciated by Glenna, but her practical side rose to the surface when she commented that a "pair of hip boots and brace of magazine revolvers" would have been more useful.[6]

In the fall, Glenna welcomed Professor Charles Gaylord Morse, a well-known authority on soil and agriculture from the Kansas State Agricultural College, to the guild's land holding. (He also happened to be the son of Artcraft Institute Guild's founder, T. Vernette Morse, and Glenna's future husband.) He had spent the previous year "making a thorough study of soils and conditions" in southern Idaho and stated, "I have personally made a test of soil, farming conditions and water rights that have come under both the government and Carey acts, and can personally vouch that they are the best investment that either the rich or poor man can take up for his own rights." After two days touring the Idaho Guild's land, Professor Morse said, "This guild has at the present time 62 acres under cultivation and considering the amount of water that has been furnished these young ladies have to show four stacks of wheat, 6 stacks of oats and 200 sacks of potatoes from three acres of land."[7]

Despite Glenna's assurances that the members of the Idaho Guild were capable of engaging in "practical farming on a large scale," the *Chicago Tribune* devoted a half page to the endeavor under the headline "A Husband or a Farm?"[8] The newspaper insisted that the women were chiefly

The *Chicago Tribune* featured Glenna and the Idaho Guild. Chicago Tribune, *November 7, 1909, in Newspapers.com.*

interested in the "possible husband crop." According to the paper, whenever Glenna, "breathless and flushed" from "[h]oisting sage on to a wagon with a pitchfork," stopped for a rest, she came face-to-face with curious male neighbors who were intrigued by her beauty and courage. Glenna, "pretty and dark eyed" while "having a head on her shoulders," admitted, "I don't think there is any girl who couldn't get a dozen husbands out there if she wanted them." But Glenna, being a practical woman, wasn't interested. "If a woman marries she loses her land, so I thought I would hang on to my land and take my chance of the husband afterwards. There is no reason why a girl can't have both if she can only withstand her offers until her claim is completed," she reportedly told the writer.[9]

In November 1909, Glenna made a trip back to Chicago to attend the National Farm-Land Congress, where the audience gathered at the Hotel La Salle to listen to speakers talk about dry farming and other new science techniques for farming in areas like southern Idaho, where the guild had purchased their spread. A newspaper reporter from the *Chicago Examiner* approached Glenna, who was eager to visit with him. "Managing a ranch is perfectly glorious and is the ideal way for the modern, self-reliant young woman to secure health, wealth and happiness. I must confess when I first considered the venture I was fearful. No girl likes to think of associating with Indians and cowboys, but dear me, how surprised I was when I got to Idaho and didn't see any Indians. People are just as civilized there as we are here," the paper reported.[10]

The following spring, Glenna returned to Chicago and taught a class on practical farming to women who spent their workdays as typewriters, potters, and bookkeepers. Having cleared the sage from the Idaho Guild's ranch, supervised men, and proved up the 160 acres, she was considered an expert. She was very clear in stating her ideas about specific roles for men and women on the ranch: "I don't think they [women] ought to try to manipulate the plows, the harrows, and the big machinery themselves, but I think they will do well to know how they should be managed and go along with their hired men to see that it is done properly. It is nonsense to say the men will not work well for a woman." She added, "As for the lighter work, such as hoeing, raking, picking fruits, weeding, feeding the cattle, driving, riding, harnessing, churning, raising chickens, I think it is beneficial to women to do it and sometimes I think they do it better than men. They have so much more patience with detail."[11]

Still, the women of the Idaho Guild, who had seen firsthand Glenna at work on their property, compared her to the men who had claims in the area. According to Glenna's partners, she put the tract "in shape while the men were still 'puttering' around over theirs."[12]

PART VII

SPREADING THE WORD

"It is only during the last three years that I have had the news to read, for my husband is so very penurious that he would never consent to subscribing for papers of any kind and that old habit of avoiding that which would give offense was so fixed that I did not dare to break it. I have always had an itching to write, and, with all my multitudinous cares, I have written, in a fitful way, for several papers, which do not pay for such matter, just because I was pleased to see my articles in print."[1]

Belle von Dorn Harbert

Helping Farm Women Save a Thousand Steps a Day between Cupboard and Table

"It means something to be a part of a great world movement, and while farm women of the world are the ones who feed the world, they do less talking about themselves, their aspirations, wrongs, troubles, hopes and plans than any other considerable number of people."[1]

BELLE VON DORN HARBERT, PRESIDENT OF THE INTERNATIONAL CONgress of Farm Women, was doing all she could to spread the word about the contributions farm women were making to the world in 1913. Through her position as head of an international organization, she represented women from all over the world and from a range of levels of society—from European royalty to the "silent peasants in Russia" and the "lonely woman in her doorway looking across the straight still prairies."[2]

Described as a "self-made woman," Belle's election to the head of the International Congress of Farm Women came about after years spent running her own farm operation in the American West.[3] As a teen in Des Moines, Iowa, she was left to support herself and landed a job as a teacher. After a few years, she became a principal. After a move to Denver, she continued teaching and earned a couple university degrees during her spare time.

But eventually Belle set aside her teaching duties and purchased a piece of farmland near Manzanola, Colorado, where she established cherry, apple, and gooseberry orchards, taking the grand prize for her

Belle von Dorn Harbert. *Library of Congress, Bain Collection, LC-B2-2874-7 [P&P].*

cherries at the 1904 St. Louis World's Fair and earning recognition for her apples at an international apple show. She became a regular exhibiter and speaker at the Colorado State Fair, giving cooking demonstrations and lectures about efficient kitchen arrangements for busy farm women. Witnessing firsthand the enthusiasm of women who attended her talks made Belle realize that farm women were passionate about interacting with their peers and were hungry for knowledge about new and efficient methods of farm-home management.

By 1911, Belle and other influential women who recognized the benefits of organizing rural women into state, national, and international groups, had established the International Congress of Farm Women. "It is a strange thing, but farmwomen, who have worked harder than any class, are the last to organize," Belle said. "We are not organizing to strike now, but to help ourselves and to uplift and upbuild."[4] At their first gathering in Colorado Springs, Colorado, in October, they confirmed their purpose for organizing: "There is a demand for the crystallization of the movement for better homes, for better sanitation, more practical education, more refinement and greater advancement morally, spiritually and mentally in the homes of the rural districts of all countries."[5]

The second annual meeting of the group was held in Lethbridge, Canada, in October 1912, where "thoughts of women from all countries mingle[d] in the solution of the problems of the home," according to Mary A. Whedon of the International Farm Women's Press Association.[6] Attendees from Palestine, India, China, Japan, and Persia heard Irma Matthews, president of the press association formed to "further the work of the congress" and open to women "connected in any editorial or reportorial way with a farm publication . . . and those engaged in minor ways as correspondents and occasional contributors," deliver a talk titled "The Farm Homes of Our Country."[7] Another speaker, Faith Felgar—the pen name for Lucretia Mullin Kepper, a reporter for the *Chicago Daily Drovers Journal* and a farmer from Iowa—told the audience that the day before arriving at the congress, she had been "preparing meals and doing the work for 25 farm hands and silo builders." Belle also was a featured speaker and told the gathering that in addition to "preparing three square meals a day, washing dishes, washing and ironing clothes, looking after a large flock of poultry, superintending the care of a cherry orchard, canning fruits, vegetables and meat," she always tried to "keep her mind in touch with the current events of the day through the magazines." According to Belle, she found time to engage in all these activities because she had invested in labor-saving devices for her home—an electric motor that ran her sewing machine, an electric iron, a coffee percolator, and an electric fireless cooker—all "at the low cost of one cent per hour." She added that "every housekeeper should be a chemist, and that the kitchen should be a laboratory holding the key to the health of her family."[8]

When the International Congress of Farm Women was convened in Ghent, Belgium, in 1913, Belle was invited to speak. "A tall, large-featured woman with silvery hair, swarthy complexion, a pair of wonderful dark eyes, and an air of friendly good fellowship," Belle delivered a "simple, straightforward talk in a manner that won the hearts" of the women who had gathered from across the globe to attend the event that was "marked by a democracy as friendly as it was noble and uplifting."[9]

When the "delegate from the American West" took to the stage, she spoke from the heart—about the most practical way to arrange a farm kitchen to save a "thousand steps a day between cupboard and table" and the value of investing in modern equipment.[10] "Money is always at hand for new labor-saving implements to be used out in the fields and their purchase has been made easy, but the farm woman had to get along with an antebellum equipment in her kitchen," Belle said. "The farmer can pay for a mower or a binder with a note; the farmer's wife has to pay cash for her tools. Mostly she doesn't know that new, more efficient kitchen equipment is on the market."[11]

The members of the international gathering listened to Belle and were enthralled, asking for more details about her recommendations and diagrams to help visualize her progressive ideas for modernizing a farm kitchen. An article reported, "They petted and lionized the American farm woman who knew how to cook, how to prune her own trees, who could quote the classics and mix the latest arsenical spray with equal facility."[12] They were so impressed that they elected Belle president of the organization.

Belle took her new duties very seriously: writing articles; speaking to farm organizations; and making plans to build a model farm home at the 1915 Panama-Pacific International Exposition in San Francisco, promising it "will be the greatest lesson in cooperation that women have ever given the world."[13] When she spoke in Tulsa, Oklahoma, in October 1914, she arrived on crutches after breaking a hip. Nothing stopped her from her mission to educate the world about the joys and trials of life as a farm woman and to campaign for support from local communities as well as the federal government. She was critical of public schools for not doing more to educate young people about the advantages of staying on the farm. And without fail, she reinforced the need for modern equipment for farm women—water, sewage, and healthy ventilation systems as well as more convenient laundry accommodations—anything to lessen the work of women on the farm. She believed it was the responsibility of women's farm organizations to speak out about these issues, "to agitate them until the world is interested in them," and to "educate the farm world so it will demand these things."[14]

Belle insisted that the value of farm women was too often overlooked and underappreciated by everyone—even farm women themselves: "The woman on the farm has never been self-conscious enough nor has she stopped her work long enough to take an inventory of her influence on humanity." Belle recognized women across the country who were experts in farm-related businesses—a Colorado woman who managed her own dairy farm and served in the state legislature; an Illinois woman who had made more than $10,000 one year from her dairy farm; a female architect and cattle farmer in New York who "puts her intelligence to test in designing labor-saving conditions . . . for the farm home."[15]

Always promoting the application of science to the work of farm women, she began to stress the need for the federal government and state universities to invest in the education of farm women: "Men have been quicker in bringing science to their aid and in shouldering their burdens on improved machinery . . . but the average farm home has not kept pace." She promised that women's groups "will be sounding brass and tinkling cymbals until the attention of science is directed toward modernizing the farm houses."[16] Belle saw the attention and money the US Department of Agriculture (USDA) gave to farmers while ignoring the needs of farm women, in her opinion. She talked about a survey and report from the

USDA titled *How the US Department of Agriculture Can Better Meet the Needs of Farm Housewives* in 1913. From letters sent out by the government agency to thousands of women across the country, it was learned that farm women felt isolated and lonely. As one writer explained, "isolation, stagnation, ignorance, loss of ambition, the incessant grind of labor, and the lack of time for improvement by reading, by social discourse, or by recreation of some sort" all coalesced to cause farm women to consider leaving the farm.[17] And Belle frequently received letters from farm women; one wrote, "I have a life to invest for the benefit of humanity, and I want to put it where it will do the most good. I believe the sisterhood of women is the basis upon which all activities must be built, but we cannot deal with farm women as a separate entry for the uplifting of humanity is the great need."[18]

As the US Congress debated the Smith-Lever Act of 1914, Belle continued her outspoken pleas for help for women from the federal government: "We are demanding a goodly share of the money spent by the government for bettering the conditions of the women on the farm ... [n]ot for selfish reasons but for the lasting benefit of humanity."[19] She very specifically laid out some demands: public restrooms in towns for the convenience of shopping farm women, experts from universities who would act as advisers to rural women in their quest for modern methods; up-to-date information about such health issues as contaminated water, mosquitoes, and flies; research for innovative, labor-saving products, such as better soap that wouldn't irritate hands and "towels of absorbent paper (at 35 cents for 150)."[20] And when the Smith-Lever Act of 1914 became law, it included a national Cooperative Extension Service "that extended outreach programs through land-grant universities to educate rural Americans about advances in agricultural practices and technology"—just what Belle had envisioned.[21]

Belle continued to advocate for her fellow farm women, always hopeful but practical in her expectations. "Perhaps someday the 'lonely farm' will cease to exist in this country, and be replaced by the village community, with its greater social advantages and opportunities," she wrote, "but that time is not in sight in the West at least."[22] In 1915, in a speech in Nebraska, Belle called for the establishment of a "bureau for farm women" at the national level. She warned that the exodus of farm families to the cities would continue if the needs of farm women were not acknowledged. She explained, "In most cases it is the discontented farm woman who induces her husband to move to the city," where she can press a "button to flood her house with light instead of having eternally to clean kerosene lamps. No carrying of water, no hauling of wood either and more social requisites." She identified the focus of the farm women's groups going forward: "Our work is to check the rush of farm people to the city by supplying social needs and household conveniences."[23]

Maria "Midy" Morgan

"She Gave Her Heart"

"MONTANA POSSESSES JUST THE RIGHT COMBINATION OF FOOD AND CLI-
mate to make perfect beef," Midy Morgan, livestock reporter for the *New
York Times*, wrote in 1882 after a tour of the western section of the United
States. She went on to add, "I am prepared to say that the Texan steer is
doomed to extinction so far as supplying the east or Europe with beef is
concerned. Now that Montana beef is accessible there will be no further
use for the cattle raised in the southwest."[1] While some ranchers, who had
witnessed changes in the Southwest landscape, grazing practices, weather
conditions, and transportation, may not have been surprised by Midy's
words, others likely questioned the claim made by a big-city reporter—
and a female at that.

But Midy Morgan had paid her dues and was one of the most
respected livestock reporters in the country. She had grown up on a large
farm in Ireland, picking up the agricultural skills she later drew from as
a livestock reporter in the United States. Midy's passion was horses, and
that's where she focused her attention. "In her youth in the old country
it was said there was no colt in Ireland so wild that she could not break
and ride it," it was once said of Midy.[2] When her dad died, the farm
went to the eldest male sibling, and Midy set out for Italy with her mom
and a sister, who studied art in Florence. Living in Rome and Florence,
Midy made the acquaintance of some wealthy and influential people
who introduced her to King Victor Emmanuel. "I am rather more than
three parts crazed on the subject of horseflesh, and I naturally wished

to be presented to King Victor Emmanuel, who is doubtless the most sporting crowned head in Europe," Midy said. The king was impressed with Midy's horse expertise and hired her to return to Ireland to purchase some horses that would be fit for royalty. It was a stressful ordeal requiring Midy to oversee the transport of the six mares she purchased in Ireland. "I knew we had thirty-two changes to make, from rail to steamer, from steamer to rail, and so on. . . . I then recollected that Hannibal had crossed the Alps . . . , and I cheered up," Midy recalled.[3] Catastrophe was averted when the train was nearly at its destination in Florence and the boxcars caught fire. Fortunately, the king's horses were spared, and he rewarded Midy with a watch with his initials encrusted in diamonds—something she treasured her entire life and left to the Metropolitan Museum of Art in her will years later.

During her two-year stay in Italy, Midy had met Americans who encouraged her to give the United States a try, and they provided her with letters of introduction to use in her job search once she arrived. Arriving

in her new homeland in June 1869, Midy immediately took a position as a chambermaid in a hotel, but she also dropped in at a few newspaper offices with her letters of introduction from her influential friends in Italy. She convinced Manton Marble, owner of the *New York World*, to hire her as a reporter. He sent her to Saratoga to cover a horse race and was pleased with the results. However, he wasn't willing to offer a permanent position, so she moved on to the *New York Times*, where she introduced herself to the editor, John Bigelow. "[S]ix feet two inches tall, garbed in rough Irish tweeds, and shod in thick-soled brogues," Midy approached the editor's desk. Boldly wielding her "deep,

Midy Morgan. Los Angeles Evening Express, *June 14, 1892, in News papers.com.*

melodious voice with an Irish lilt," Midy announced, "I am Maria Morgan. I want a job."[4] When Mr. Bigelow explained the only position available was livestock reporter, she said, "I can fill it."[5] By some accounts, Bigelow had little faith that Midy would survive the rough-and-tumble world of the livestock pens or the New York journalism scene. "Oh! She'll not hold the place a week," he said.[6] But he was wrong—Midy established herself over the next twenty years as a formidable journalist for the *Times* and agricultural publications such as the Buffalo *Live Stock Journal, Farm and Fireside, Field and Farm, American Agriculturist, Country Gentleman,* and *Spirit of the Times.*

"[S]he revels in sheep and cows, has a penchant for pigs, and adores horses," a Mississippi newspaper reported in 1870. She had "broad and substantial shoulders," and "her ankles are not fairylike," while she "ambles along upon a sole of prodigious generosity."[7] Her job required her to spend days at the stockyards mingling amid the cattle, hogs, and horses and getting to know the cattlemen. She started at dawn, greeting livestock cars arriving by rail. Dressed in hip-length rubber waders and waterproof coats on wet or snowy days, her hair "bunched in a waterfall," she was known to carry a six-shooter.[8] When she returned to the office, she oftentimes arrived chewing a piece of straw, storming past the desks of her male colleagues "like a tornado."[9]

At first Midy was the object of ridicule and jokes, but in time, she "won the respectful admiration of all the stock dealers, butchers, drovers and railway men of her acquaintance" and became known as a "lady who would report the exact condition of the cattle, sheep, hog, and horse markets" and "could neither be bought nor sold in the interests of any clique of stock dealers."[10] Her deep knowledge of livestock markets and animal science, in addition to her passion for accuracy and curiosity for news, overshadowed her critics. "Eccentric though she was in many ways, she did more to show what intellectual and business capabilities a woman possesses in an unusual field than almost any other newspaper reporter of her sex," a fellow journalist said about Midy.[11]

When Midy took her tour of the western states in 1882, she had been writing for more than a decade. Her articles in agricultural publications about proper treatment of animals were well known by ranchers and cattlemen. Her recipe for hair growth in horses, a formula she had personally used with success on the tails and manes of her own animals, consisted of corrosive sublimate, oxymuriate of mercury, and distilled water applied to the area where hair was thin. If the hair was rubbed off by the "animal's own endeavors," then a concoction of flour sulfur, pulverized saltpeter, and fresh butter or fresh-rendered hog's lard applied three or four times should eliminate any skin irritation, according to Midy.[12] Of course, at times a horse's well-being was affected by its owner and resulted in unfavorable behavior on the part of the animal. She didn't hesitate to place blame where it belonged. "We commence on a broad basis, by saying that stable viciousness is generally caused by ill-treatment," she wrote. A poorly fitted saddle could make a horse's back tender; demanding overexertion may cause a horse to balk at a harness. "Horses run away in nearly all cases from injudicious treatment. They are kept shivering in the cold or stung to fury in the heat, till their patience is exhausted, or they are frightened by harness giving way or by a load running on them, or they are tortured to madness by severe bits and cruelly tight check reins," Midy warned.[13]

Writing in the *Century Magazine* in November 1881, Midy offered "Hints to Horseback Riders." "Not a little of the comfort and safety of the rider depends on the excellence of the paraphernalia of his turn-out," she wrote. And to acquire a first-rate saddle, she encouraged dealing only with a "first-class maker." She added, "Without a feeling of comfort there can be no grace in the saddle, and an ungraceful rider had better walk."[14]

In 1879, Midy warned that American cattlemen were suffering in terms of trade with foreign markets. Because of extremely stringent quarantine restrictions in England—which did not apply to Irish or Scottish animals—American cattle producers suffered losses when selling to England. However, Midy reported, Irish sheep were not as favorable to the English, as recent shipments had been "in the last stage of disease of the liver" and "very little of the meat is at all fit for human food"— despite being specially treated by the sellers through special seasonings "to remove the unpleasant odor and taste."[15]

By 1882, when Midy embarked on her western tour of cattle country, she intended to learn more about the cattle producers and their stock

Chicago Stockyards in 1905. *Library of Congress, LC-USZ62-55745.*

as well as to explore options for shipping of dressed beef. Traveling by rail, Midy's first stop was Chicago, where she toured the famous Union Stockyards. During nearly a month in the West, Midy came away with some very strong opinions, which she eagerly shared. On her return trip, she stopped in St. Paul, Minnesota, and gave an interview to a newspaper reporter, and in December, the *New York Times* ran her article

"Miss Middy Morgan's Views of the Facilities and Products of the Cattle Ranches of the Northwest." She almost certainly caused some controversy among livestock producers in various sections of the country with her words.

"The sources of supply for beef cattle is moving rapidly to the northwest, and Texas and the surrounding country are losing their former importance," Midy wrote. "Persons who are familiar with the cattle trade know that the Texas animals are very poor stock." According to Midy, Colorado and Wyoming cattle were superior to Texas animals, yet none could compare to Montana's. "In Montana evidence abounds of the advantages derivable from judicious and careful breeding. The herds of that State have been bred with great care from the start, and they are of rare excellence," Midy wrote.[16]

Midy expressed her delight in the fresh meat she ate in Montana. "I never tasted better beef," she wrote. "It was simply delicious, with a certain wild or gamey flavor which was exquisite." And she believed the meat easterners consumed couldn't compare to the fresh fare she'd had in Montana: "Now I saw these Montana steers loaded upon the cars at Miles City, and sleek, short-legged, straight-backed fellows they were, averaging not less than 1,100 pounds each; and I mourned as I imagined that I saw them unloaded in New York or New Jersey, tired, jaded and feverish with their terrible journey." Of course, that long, stressful journey from the Montana cattle ranches to the eastern butchers' stalls caused the meat to become a "flabby, lifeless, stringy substance," in Midy's words. She believed the best method to ensure fresh, delectable beef anywhere in the country was to "slaughter the cattle as near as may be to their ranges" and then ship the meat in refrigerators.[17] And she believed that would not be far in the future.

In 1890, writing in the *American Agriculturist*, Midy posed the question, "When shall we get better beef?" She placed part of the responsibility on American consumers who "prefer sirloin steak and rib-roast from worn-out oxen and diseased Texas steers to flanks and chucks of healthy, corn-fed, grade beeves." She again cited long train rides from the West to eastern markets as a cause for distasteful meat. And she had a dire warning for any sausage lover who would have his "gastronomic pleasures seriously interfered with" if he "observed the sources from which flow his tidbits": "old oxen and worn-out dairy cows."[18]

Midy died only two years later from complications from a fall on ice at the Jersey City stockyards. At the time, a fellow female reporter said, "By her years of solid, magnificent work she helped to advance the belief in women's capacity a hundred years."[19] And in her obituary in June 1892, the *New York Times*, her employer for more than twenty years, described her as "one of the first women to take up daily newspaper work" and in whose work "whether it took the form of dry market reports or description or expert analysis, she gave her heart."[20]

Kate Field

Promoting American Wine

"MISS KATE FIELD HAS BEEN ENGAGED BY THE VITICULTURISTS OF CALifornia to preach the gospel of grape juice to the drinkers of corn juice in the East," the *Weekly Mercury* newspaper of Oroville, California, announced in August 1888. "[S]he will endeavor to convince the staid, old corn-soaked East, that California grape juice is not intoxicating, in fact, that its use will encourage temperance and supplant whiskey."[1] It would be her duty to encourage temperance in drink—substituting beer and whiskey with "light California wines."[2]

Kate's reputation as an actress, speaker, writer, and activist was already cemented in American literary circles, and her new position as a spokesperson for the wine industry complemented her opposition to total abstinence of alcoholic beverages. Kate made clear her feelings about the distinctions between temperance and total abstinence: "[I]f there is one craze more reprehensible than all others to me it is the craze of prohibition." She touted the advantages of using wine with moderation and in specific settings—including with meals, "where it not only cheers and makes bad food good and good food better, but assists digestion."[3]

However, at a time when prohibition movements swept the nation at federal, state, and local levels, Kate's association with antiprohibition forces pitted her against groups that viewed her work for the California Viticultural Commission disgraceful and unbecoming a woman of her stature. But it was her status in society that made her attractive to California grape growers and wine producers as they looked for ways

KATE FIELD: A RARE AND HITHERTO UNPUBLISHED PORTRAIT

Kate Field. National Magazine, *January 1906.*

to introduce native beverages to Americans who favored only imported wines—especially those from France.

"She is a woman with a social standing, and will be able to reach the people we want to reach—the leaders in society, who make customs and set fashions," Arpad Haraszthy, president of the California Viticultural Commission, explained. He warned that while Kate was a unique and valued emissary to convey the commission's message, she would face challenges: "She will have two popular prejudices to combat. One is against wine itself by those who confound wine-drinking with rum-drinking and bar-tippling, and the other is the prejudice against native labels among those who think that all good wines cross the Atlantic."[4]

None of it was a deterrent for Kate, who replied to her invitation to represent the commission, "I thoroughly appreciate the compliment you pay to me in thinking that I can advance the cause of California's noblest industry. . . . Believing most profoundly that the only road to true temperance is by the substitution of light pure wines and beers . . . I therefore accept the proposition . . . and will preach the gospel of the grape to the best of my ability."[5]

Born in 1840 in St. Louis, Kate spent her childhood and young-adult years in New England and Europe, where she studied art and music. Over the years, she developed her performance and writing skills, earning a living with both. According to a biographer, "She had the happy faculty of combining the two generally distinct arts of acting and writing."[6] She attended events where she interacted with the likes of Charles Dickens, Oscar Wilde, and Mark Twain. Alexander Graham Bell asked Kate to help demonstrate his telephone to England's Queen Victoria in 1878 by singing the Irish folk song "Kathleen Mavourneen" over the phone, to enjoyment of the queen.

In time, she came to rely on her writing and lecture tours as her primary sources of income. Her articles appeared in newspapers and magazines, and for a few years she produced her own publication, *Kate Field's Washington*, a sixteen-page weekly sold at newsstands and at the finest hotels in Washington, D.C., or through subscription for two dollars per year. Her passions and causes covered a wide range of topics. Often controversial, frequently thought provoking, Kate's work drew reactions.

In response to her frustration with the cost of clothing for women, she founded the Co-operative Dress Association in 1880 with a storefront on Twenty-Third Street in New York City, where, with a membership fee of twenty-five dollars per share, stockholders enjoyed discounted prices for clothing and other objects.[7]

After living among people of the Mormon religion in Utah for several months in 1885, Kate embarked on a lecture tour about her interpretation of what she had witnessed. She charged a dollar for audiences to hear her sensational charges against Mormonism, including "Secret Oaths, Tithing, Missionaries, Schools, Blood Atonement, Polygamy, Politics and Rebellion."[8]

She petitioned Congress to remove duties on works of art, and after a visit to Alaska, she advocated for territory status for the region. After a short visit to San Diego, California, her comments about the citizens of that city couldn't have earned her any followers there. "Lunatics are an intensely interesting study to me," Kate remarked, "and 30,000 of them at large, going about as though endowed with reason, so irresistibly attracted me that I sailed for Los Angeles."[9]

It wasn't surprising that those remarks earned Kate some pushback. A reporter from the *St. Louis Post-Dispatch* described Kate "as polished as a glacier, and as evasive as an eel," with a smile "like pale sunlight on a midwinter day"—someone who "never fails to make you feel that she is a cat and you are a mouse, and that she is getting a thousand times more amusement out of you than you will ever get information out of her."[10] And as she began her speaking tours for the California Viticultural Commission, prohibition groups across the country responded. In the fall of 1888, Woman's Christian Temperance Union (WCTU) groups in Massachusetts, Delaware, Kansas, and Dakota Territory passed resolutions denouncing Kate: "We deplore the action of Miss Kate Field in agreeing to lecture under pay of wine growers of California in favor of beer and wine as a beverage, and urge the national WCTU to provide a speaker to reply to her."[11]

Despite dissatisfaction with Kate's behavior from some, the California Viticultural Commission was pleased with the work she was doing for the organization. "The members of the Viticultural Commission are very

CHAPTER 18

enthusiastic over Miss Field's labors in preaching the gospel of the grape, seeing one of the most valuable results in the attention she has drawn to the subject and the discussion of it provoked," the *San Francisco Chronicle* reported in March 1889.[12] The growers group paid her a salary of $250 per month to spread the word about their delightful products, and when she requested an additional $500 for a speaking engagement in New York City to introduce California wines to "Eastern homes," the organization provided it.[13]

In Boston in 1889, she delivered a speech titled "The Intemperance of Prohibition," where she related an incident that had prompted her to take on the antiprohibition cause. On a visit to Iowa, she had been informed that prohibition was in place, and therefore, when she visited a local drugstore to obtain a "half-pint of California brandy for medicinal purposes," she was sold a bottle of something labeled "French brandy." After getting quite sick from the remedy, she asked a chemist to analyze the concoction, and it was found to contain "fusel oil." She told the audience, "A man selling such stuff for medicine ought to be prosecuted for manslaughter." In Kate's opinion, this was another sign that prohibition was not working as intended. She recounted another incident when she tried to purchase a broom in Kansas City, Kansas, and was asked by the store clerk if she wanted it "with or without." When she expressed confusion, the clerk unscrewed the handle of the broom and showed her a pint bottle filled with whiskey concealed in the handle. When he remarked that the price was the same with or without, she said she'd take the "with." However, she found the contents to be "very poor whiskey."[14]

When William Harrison ran on the Republican ticket for president in 1888, he promised to protect American industries from foreign competition. Kate, always looking for an opportunity to promote domestic wines—specifically California wines—wrangled a meeting with the inaugural planning committee in late 1888. Her message in March 1889: "[A]n administration founded on the principle of 'protection to American industry' should have none but domestic wines on the table at its inaugural banquet."[15] However, the inaugural committee decided against following Kate's advice.

In March 1889, she was back in Washington, D.C., where she delivered a lecture at a reception for several hundred "scientists, Congressmen,

Constables of the Des Moines searchers and advance guard of the Fighting Prohibition Army who used various means to fight violators of prohibition laws in Iowa. *Library of Congress Prints and Photographs Division, Washington, D.C., LC-USZ62-24748.*

politicians, journalists and literary and society men." She had invited the new president and his cabinet—none of whom responded. However, the audience of influential policy makers who did attend enjoyed refreshments from California vineyards as they listened to Kate talk about "how I came to write my lecture," "history of stimulants," "alcohol as a food," personal liberty, and "prohibition public school textbooks."[16]

In her series of lectures for the Viticultural Commission, Kate explained her opposition to prohibition: "I was offended by the hypocrisy and falsehood which I saw in the liquor traffic . . . double doors and roundabout passageways to the hotel bars and fictitious names for strong drinks. I think that the use of pure, mild wines at table with no drinking

115

William Harrison ran for president promising to protect American industries. *Library of Congress, LC-DIG-pga-03586, Joseph A. Burrows.*

between meals, would greatly promote temperance in this country. It certainly would be a great gain for temperance if mild California wines took the place of whisky for general use."[17] Additionally, according to Kate, not only were California wines superior to all others, but they were also cheaper than beer.

By the time Kate died in 1896 in Hawaii while campaigning for annexation of the islands, her life's work had provoked varied reactions. Critics described her as possessing a "sharp and often a caustic tongue" and "severe in her utterances."[18] An admirer described Kate as "shrewd, spirited, clever, independent, audacious and not over-sensitive," adding "she rarely bridles her tongue or her pen."[19] Even her critics recognized endearing qualities in Kate, writing that "she makes ample amends by the rare generosity of her acts" and "she is kind in deed as she is often unkind in expression."[20] Her obituaries, including one in the *New York Times*, recalled her accomplishments as an actress, writer, businesswoman, lecturer, and activist. Her contributions to the American wine industry were said to have "enriched and enlarged the vineyards of America."[21] Members of the Columbia Historical Society, an organization formed in 1894 by Kate and other individuals committed to "gathering and preserving the history of the national capital," proclaimed that "America is richer, more cultured, and nobler, and the world is better because of Kate Field's life."[22]

Part VIII

Stock Women

"I use an old fashioned churn, and the process of churning occupies from thirty minutes to three hours ... and I always read something while churning, and though that may look like a poor way to attain self-culture, yet if your reading is of the nature to bring about that desirable result, one will surely be greatly benefited by these daily exercises. . . . [M]y reading has always been for the purpose of becoming well informed; and when knitting stockings for the family I always have a book or paper in reading distance; or, if I have a moment to rest or to wait on something, I pick up something and read during the time. I even take a paper with me to the fields and read while I stop for rest."[1]

Changunak Antisarlook Andrewuk

The Reindeer Queen

On a frigid Arctic night in February 1923, a school superintendent, a couple teachers, a government nurse, and a freelance writer from
Washington State found themselves sharing tight quarters in a remote
cabin in western Alaska, thanks to the hospitality of a queen. The travelers had embarked on a hundred-mile cross-country journey from St.
Michael by reindeer-drawn sleds to Shaktoolik to attend a fair. Expecting
to camp out in the open the first night, the group was sidetracked when
the sleds carrying their camping equipment were delayed. Fortunately,
they were offered a place to stay by a local celebrity—Changunak Antisarlook Andrewuk—also known as the Reindeer Queen, or more commonly Sinrock Mary.

Mary invited the superintendent and the women to spread their
sleeping bags on her cabin floor. And after a restful night, the group was
treated with a hot breakfast from "Queen Mary's warm kitchen." If the
walls of Mary's cabin could have talked about the conversations that took
place that night, they may have told of a lively exchange of ideas and
life experiences by the diverse personalities who had unexpectedly shared
a few hours. Mary, an Iñupiat who spoke Russian, a little English, and
more than one Native dialect, may have captured the spotlight with stories about her life as a reindeer herder and businesswoman. Of course, the
walls couldn't talk, so future generations were left with only a hint of what
happened during those hours. In the words of the writer in the group,
Nona Marquis Snyder, "that night at 'Sinrock Mary's' deserves a chapter

Changunak Antisarlook Andrewuk. *Ickes Collection, Anchorage Museum, B1975.175.158.*

all to itself, so many interesting things occurred—and I cannot even begin it here."[1] Although details of the chance encounter may never be known, Sinrock Mary's life as a successful businesswoman has become legendary.

Mary's early years, as the daughter of an Iñupiat woman and a Russian trader, were spent at St. Michael on Norton Sound, a lively trading post where ships arrived carrying supplies and people from all over. She learned the ways of her people from her mother, who taught her to fish, hunt, sew, and tan hides, and she met people from other cultures and learned new languages. Those early encounters laid the foundation for her future.

In 1889, Mary married an Iñupiat trader, Charlie Antisarlook. The couple shared a traditional Iñupiat life together—hunting, fishing, and trading with people who arrived on the ships that entered the ports during the summertime. On one of those encounters, the couple met a couple of influential men who opened new opportunities for Mary and Charlie.

———

"Richard Price steward severely stabbed another seaman . . . and threatened the life of the First Mate. . . . Price confined in single irons . . . afraid to keep the man aboard his vessel and asked permission to transfer him to the 'Bear.'"[2]

"Engine at half speed, with jibs, staysails and topsail set."[3]

"Crew sweeping for lost anchor."[4]

Typical entries in a ship's logs in the 1890s recorded daily events, written in longhand by an officer. There was the occasional altercation or incident where a seaman went missing after a shore leave, but most entries recited the day-to-day maintenance and operation of the ship. Such was the case with the logs of the US Revenue Marine cutter the USS *Bear*, under the command of Captain Michael A. Healy in the summer of 1890 as the vessel set sail from Seattle to Alaska. The son of an Irish plantation owner and a former enslaved woman, Healy had earned the name "Hell Roaring Mike" but had also become well known and respected as the face of the US government in Alaska.[5] On Friday, May 9, 1890, at four o'clock, the *Bear*'s log indicated, "Dr. Sheldon Jackson, came on board for passage to Point Barrow and return by authority of Department."[6] Jackson had

Mary and her husband with other family members. *Library of Congress, LC-DIG-ppmsc-02348.*

been tasked with setting up the Bureau of Education in northwest Alaska and needed bilingual locals to help with census taking. So when the *Bear* completed coaling in Seattle and began its journey with a light westerly breeze and clear skies, Healy knew he would be adding passengers along the way.

Early on the morning of Friday, July 4, 1890, with a "[g]entle breeze and cloudy" skies, the *Bear* entered Port Clarence, Alaska, where the ship "[t]ook on board . . . for passage to Cape Prince of Wales . . . Indian interpreters Charley [*sic*] and his wife Mary to act as interpreters in taking census and establishing schools."[7] As it turned out, Captain Healy and Jackson shared a dream to introduce reindeer herding to Alaska. During his travels to Siberia, the captain had met very successful Chukchi reindeer herders, and Jackson believed that Alaskan Natives should not become overly dependent on the uncertainties of hunting and fishing. Together, the two men worked to facilitate a project where reindeer would be brought from Siberia and Native Alaskans would be trained as herders.

With the combined support of private investors and various government agencies, Healy and Jackson embarked on their ambitious venture.

Mary traveled to Siberia to help negotiate the purchase of a herd, and in July 1892, 171 reindeer arrived at the newly built Teller Reindeer Station in Port Clarence, where Charlie was waiting to begin his apprenticeship as a reindeer herder. Mary and Charlie were given special privileges—including a log house to live in at the station—and Charlie was promised a salary, to be paid in reindeer rather than money. But it wasn't until 1894 that Charlie and Mary acquired their herd. Under the project guidelines, they were lent one hundred animals for a period of five years, after which they had to repay the government for the original reindeer. The idea was that they would grow the herd well beyond the initial one hundred. Charlie signed an official agreement, and early in 1895, he and Mary took their newly acquired herd of 115 reindeer to a location on the Sinuk River, usually pronounced "Sinrock," which was how Mary acquired her name "Sinrock Mary."[8]

Those early years of herding were visited by setbacks. In 1898, Sheldon Jackson pressed Charlie to repay his debt after only two years. Jackson, who had been appointed to his position by the US secretary of the interior and worked for the government, also was a Christian missionary, and he was not shy about letting those two roles overlap. He took 121 reindeer from Charlie and Mary's herd and dropped them off at a couple missions. The same year, the government convinced Charlie and Mary to come to the aid of a whaling ship crew who had become frozen in an ice pack at Point Barrow, where the crew were reportedly starving. According to the agreement with the government, the couple would receive "ample and suitable reward" in return for lending the herd to the humanitarian cause, and Charlie would receive a salary for traveling with the herd to Point Barrow. Using eighteen sleds, 438 reindeer were moved to save the starving whalers seven hundred miles away.[9] But it was all a misunderstanding: The whalers weren't starving, and the reindeer were delivered to two missions in the area. Mary and Charlie were paid back for their efforts—but not until 1900, the same year Charlie died.

Over the next forty-eight years, Mary worked to build her inheritance of around three hundred reindeer into a thriving business. She was faced with challenges along the way. With her beautiful Iñupiat features, generous spirit, and that precious reindeer herd worth a great deal of money, she became a target for unscrupulous as well as well-meaning individuals. Gold prospectors targeted Mary's herd for food and transportation. Dishonest ones shot at the reindeer in attempts to scatter the herd and steal an animal. Others purchased her reindeer—for $150 per animal—to use as pack animals.[10] She spurned marriage offers and dealt with a couple of costly lawsuits—one from a couple of Charlie's brothers, who believed they should have inherited the herd upon his death. Another suit dragged over two years, when a fellow who had helped drive the herd from one location to another for Mary sued her for wages. The court ruled in Mary's favor, possibly because the jury learned that the fellow had sold off some of the herd while in transit and pocketed the profits.

In August 1902, Mary married Andrew Andrewuk, who turned out to be a good match. She continued to operate the reindeer business, while Andrew lent his support to her work, until he died in 1918. By then, Mary had moved the herd to Klikitarik, between St. Michael and Unalakleet, and made a living selling meat to families, store merchants, and trading and military posts. Her home at Unalakleet was a gathering place for friends and a home for her eleven adopted kids. Although she hired people to fulfill the day-to-day duties associated with the herd, she visited the animals on a regular basis. At the time of her death, she owned an estimated 1,500 animals, making it the biggest herd in Alaska for a time and earning her the title "Reindeer Queen."[11]

Katherine Pearson

"Ostrich Queen of the Western Hemisphere"

"The ostrich is as senseless a bird as exists. So far as I am able to judge they are absolutely and entirely without brains."[1]

KATHERINE PEARSON'S UNFLATTERING ASSESSMENT OF THE LONG-legged, gangly necked bird inhabiting her Arizona ranch may have been a bit harsh. However, the birds' brains were of lesser interest to this shrewd businesswoman than were their feathers that fashionable women across the globe cherished for their hats and boas and that practical-minded housewives utilized in their feather dusters. She'd been in the business of breeding these curious-looking creatures for nearly a decade, so she knew something about their personalities and living habits as well as their value in the marketplace.

In the late 1890s, Katherine and her husband, Aylma Y. "A. Y." Pearson, began searching for interesting new business ventures in states with weather less harsh than New York's for Aylma's consumption. He had been a very successful theater manager, and the couple had a bit of money to invest. In 1899, they bought land in Jacksonville, Florida, where they operated an ostrich farm and aviary stocked with pheasants, snowy aigrettes, ducks, geese, swans, flamingoes, pelicans, and herons imported from India, China, and other lands. But the Pearsons found the Florida weather a bit too damp for Aylma, and they looked toward the Southwest. With land in Arizona Territory selling for between $40 and $125 per acre, depending on location and distance from a canal, they decided to take what they had learned in their Florida enterprise and set up an ostrich ranch about ten miles west of the town of Phoenix, population 5,500.

The Pearsons established the Phoenix-American Ostrich Company with 250 birds in November 1899. The hot, dry Arizona weather was perfect for ostrich raising and just what the doctor ordered for A. Y.'s stubborn health problems. A. Y. was confident in the new venture and believed they had an advantage over importers from Africa and South America. "Ostrich raising is a matter of business now with my family, and we believe we shall have no difficulty in competing with the importers of feathers. In fact there can be little competition. The importation of feathers into the United States amounts annually to $3,000,000, exclusive of a 50 per cent tariff. . . . [W]e, of course, will escape the tariff," he said.[2]

By 1902, the Phoenix-American Ostrich Company had become a tourist attraction, where for twenty-five cents, visitors could wander the grounds and observe the exotic birds as they squatted on the ground with their wings spread to show off their plumage or watch a male bird "weave his sinuous neck about in threatening curves" while emitting a "hoarse sort of croaking hiss."[3] The ranch was quite a showcase, with rows and rows of bird pens laid out like houses on a city street. The Pearsons were proud of the unusual business they had staked out in the desert.

Despite Arizona's favorable weather, A. Y.'s health declined. "My husband was becoming more feeble every day. I tried to do my duty and as a result I learned all the inns [sic] and outs in breeding birds and selling feathers," Katherine said.[4] And when A. Y. died in 1903, she was left to handle the family business.

From the start, the Pearsons had relied on their farm workers and managers to carry out the day-to-day operations of the ranch. Katherine continued to rely on them to plant, irrigate, and harvest the fields of alfalfa and to maintain the miles of high, wire fences containing the birds and protecting them from wolves and dogs. The machinery used to prepare the birds' nutritional diet needed regular upkeep and repairs, the brooder houses required cleaning, and incubators demanded constant monitoring to ensure consistent temperatures for the precious eggs. And most importantly, workers devoted a great deal of time to those unintelligent,

Phoenix American Ostrich Farm

MRS. A. Y. PEARSON, Proprietor.

Winter Opening, Thursday, Dec. 1st.

EXHIBITION AND CITY SALES ROOMS end of Capitol addition car line.
Interesting collection of Ostriches of all ages from the tiny chicks to full plumaged birds.

Beautiful display of selected feather goods and souvenir novelties AT PRODUCERS PRICES.

In connection with the above we are pleased to announce a new departure of interest to the ladies. Mrs. M. C. Close of New York City will present

A FULL LINE OF PATTERN HATS

Copied from the most exclusive New York and Parisian models.
Take Washington street car going west.

Katherine promoted her ostrich farm with tours. Arizona Republic, *November 22, 1904.*

finicky, at times combative, feathery creatures who ruled the roost at the Pearson ranch.

At every stage of the ostrich-raising process, Katherine, with the help of her employees, was consumed with protecting her substantial investment—starting with the care of the large eggs produced by the females. Both female and male birds took turns sitting on the nests—females took the day shift; males, night. However, the males could be irresponsible, and the females were reluctant to cover night shifts, according to Katherine. She explained, "If for any reason his lordship gets sulky he goes off on strike, and the female being equally independent—the nest is left to take care of itself."[5] Female ostriches were notorious for carelessly dropping eggs in unexpected locations, requiring workers to search for and gather the delicate commodities each day. An "egg telescope" was used to differentiate the fertilized from the unfertilized eggs.[6] Fertilized eggs were taken to the incubators, where they remained for about forty days in specially designed trays large enough to hold the five-inch-diameter, seven-inch-long eggs. The unfertilized eggs were set aside to sell as curiosities.

Lax parenting skills continued after the baby birds' arrival. "The parents seem to be perfectly indifferent to their fate," Katherine said. "Unless the young birds are taken from them as soon as hatched there is great danger of their being trampled to death."[7] Baby birds, with their speckled and striped feathers, quickly learned to fend for themselves, eating a special concoction of ground alfalfa and wheat bran. Within six months, the birds were subject to their first clipping, and typically, a clipping took place every eight months after that. Katherine insisted the birds experienced no physical pain from the clipping and plucking procedure. However, she had observed her birds suffering psychological effects. "When they are first plucked they become very sulky and seem to wish to hide themselves," she noted. "If a plucked bird is turned with the unplucked they fall on him tooth and nail and the poor fellow is made to suffer for his loss."[8]

When the young birds were ready to "assume the responsibilities of conjugal existence" at about three and a half years, workers rounded them up from the pastures and drove them into the rows of pens.[9] Because the male birds became quite combative during mating time and commonly injured each other if placed side by side in adjoining pens, the Pearsons devised a simple solution—leaving alternate pens empty. Typically, ostriches were faithful to their mates for life, but occasionally a male took a second mate. And, according to Katherine's observations, she had "known the widowed bird to accept a second mate, but not until after several years."[10]

Of course, the purpose of breeding was to ensure a steady supply of birds that produced mounds and mounds of feathers for market. Ostrich meat was considered a viable food source for humans, and one scrambled ostrich egg equaled about two and a half dozen chicken eggs. The feathers were taken from different parts of the bird's body—wings, body, and legs. There were about twenty-four plumes on each wing. After clipping, workers took the plumes to a grading table, where they were grouped by lengths of feathers. The average ostrich produced about one and a half pounds of feathers each year—from thirty to fifty dollars' worth. The shortest drab feathers used in feather dusters were worth about four dollars per pound. The quality of the feathers increased with each cutting, so as the birds aged, they became more valuable. Males' plumes were glossy black and white, and the females', a "quiet gray and brown."[11] Nubian birds' plumes were naturally curled, and their neck feathers were pink. By the time women wore hats decorated with ostrich feathers or cleaned their homes with feather dusters, the feathers had been washed and bleached many times by the manufacturers who purchased Katherine's raw feathers.

Ostriches were known for their longevity. Katherine always claimed she had never seen a grown bird that was not healthy and that in ten years of farming, the Pearsons had not lost a single bird to disease. "While in

Katherine Pearson's farm featured in news article. Omaha Daily Bee, *May 26, 1907.*

Arizona and Florida we never lost a grown bird except through accident," she said.[12] Because a bird could be expected to produce for generations, the cost to purchase one was steep—according to Katherine, $100 for very young South African birds, $150 for Nubians, and hundreds more for older imported breeders.

"Since my husband's death I have increased the Phoenix flock to 980 breeders and the acreage to 2,000 making it the largest breeding farm in America," Katherine told a newspaper reporter in 1907. She had expanded her operation to Cuba, where she believed the climate would be conducive to successful ostrich farming. Because the new venture was in the experimental stage, she limited the number of birds to forty-five on her twenty-seven acres of land near a "beautiful old Spanish castle."[13] Still, it was a risky investment. She had paid $1,500 per pair for Nubians shipped from France. Fortunately, although the trip had taken more than a month, all the birds survived, and none had been injured.

When Katherine met her first ostriches back in the 1890s, she envisioned becoming attached to them as pets but quickly realized that was unlikely. "When I found that they could not be taught to cross the road and that the ones we see in harness have to be driven between two lines of wire fencing to prevent them from bolting I was convinced there was no use in trying to train them for the house," she said.[14] And over the years, she came to regard the odd creatures simply as sources of revenue. "As a business I understand and enjoy raising feathers, but so far as the personality of the ostrich is concerned—why, they haven't any sense; they are utterly silly. They are just big, healthy idiots in the shape of birds," she said.[15]

Mary Ann Dyer Goodnight

Saving the Buffalo

"The revolting cruelty of the hide-hunting years was shocking in the extreme. On every hand, my aunt told me, there was evidence of the merciless destruction. Hideous waste and rankest heartlessness were stalking hand in hand over the breadths of prairie and the lonely canyons of west Texas."[1]

ANNIE DYER NUNN ECHOED THE WORDS OF HER AUNT, MARY ANN DYER Goodnight, owner of what was believed to be the "Only [Buffalo] Herd in the World Owned by a Woman."[2] A "woman ahead of her time" for her efforts to conserve one of the country's precious natural resources, Mary Goodnight witnessed the disturbing plight of the buffalo firsthand as she established a ranch with her husband, Charles, in the 1870s in the Texas Panhandle.[3] She knew something about tenacity and determination, having endured one of the "longest courtships on the Texas frontier" before finally marrying her husband in 1870 after a five-year engagement and a nearly ten-year relationship.[4] She had been a teacher in Black Springs and Weatherford, Texas, during her courtship, and when she agreed to marry Charles, it was with the condition that they wed in Hickman, Kentucky, where she had relatives, and that her three orphan brothers join the newlyweds in their move to a ranch in Pueblo, Colorado. They must have seemed like reasonable conditions to the man who had waited for years to marry the "pretty, black-haired girl" who would remain his wife for more than fifty years.[5] And she proved to be just as "brave and daring" as Charles.[6]

After seven years ranching in the Pueblo area, Mary and her husband set out for the Palo Duro Canyon of Texas, where the US Army had driven out Comanche, Kiowa, and Cheyenne Indians to make way for Anglo settlers.[7] Initially, they went into partnership with John and Cornelia Adair to establish the JA Ranch in 1877. The journey from Pueblo to the bottom of the canyon, where the Goodnights had found the best environment for their cattle, was a harrowing experience. They traveled with eight wagons loaded with building materials and enough flour, sugar, bacon, and dried fruit to last a few months. Mary drove one of the wagons covered with sheeting to give some protection from the elements. When the caravan reached the cap of the canyon, the travelers realized it was impossible to drive the wagons down the steep incline. So the wagons were dismantled, and the parts and all the supplies were loaded onto mules, who carried everything to a point where the wagons were reassembled, reloaded, and driven the last ten miles down the canyon to the ranch site.

When the travelers camped for the night, unfamiliar sounds echoing within the canyon walls kept Mary awake. Torrential rains with lightning—a "blaze of light with constant flashes on the wagon sheet"—and "hoarse rumbling from the throats of thousands of buffaloes" reverberated within the canyon walls.[8] "It was enough to frighten the bravest woman and I am sure few women would have been as calm as my wife during a time like that," Charles recalled.[9] While his wife may have feared the very real possibility of a deadly stampede of the majestic, bellowing creatures, she also steadfastly and confidently resolved to save these national treasures from extinction.

Those early days on the JA Ranch were difficult in some respects for Mary, who missed female companionship and some of the comforts of her home in Colorado. But she also thrived in this new environment, where she "[m]ade friends and companions of the wildflowers" and "enjoyed the music of the insects and birds" while she "gloried in the towering walls and the gorgeous colorings of the canyon."[10] Her new home was a three-room log cabin snugly chinked with red clay, kept toasty warm by a fireplace in each room, and brightened with paned windows painstakingly transported in the wagons from Pueblo. Mary gathered water

Mary Ann Dyer Goodnight. *Panhandle-Plains Historical Museum, Canyon, Texas.*

from a nearby spring and stored it in a barrel near the cabin door. She swept the dirt floors and tended her chickens and flowers, safe from marauding wildlife and thriving within the cedar fence encircling the cabin. Through her precious paned windows, Mary relished views of towering bluffs and a river running along the north side of the cabin. Cowboys who helped with the Goodnights' cattle bunked in one room of the cabin, and she made them meals in the middle room that served as kitchen and dining room. But Mary's day-to-day activities extended beyond typical housework. She also tended the couple's cattle, sometimes driving the herds with the cowboys and her husband and brothers to Dodge City for sales. She rode sidesaddle on a specially designed saddle atop her horse, Patty, a "handsome, well gaited, and fast" mount.[11]

Mary never forgot the cries of the buffaloes that had kept her awake on her journey to her new home in Texas, and as she continued to witness the massive destruction of the vast buffalo herds in the wild, she was haunted by the sounds of young animals left to fend for themselves.[12] "For weeks and months the cry of starving buffalo calves rang in Mrs. Goodnight's ears. And that pitiful wail not only reached her ears, but it reached her heart," Phebe K. Warner, a columnist for the *Fort Worth Star-Telegram*, wrote. And she made the decision to do something about it—turning to her husband and brother to help carry out her plan. According to Phebe, Mary petitioned her husband, "Charley, if you and Lee will go out and rope some of those little starving calves and bring them to the corral I'll feed them and raise them."[13] So Charley delivered three little orphan buffaloes to Mary's doorstep, and she began her journey to save the buffalo. "Mrs. Goodnight had fixed her mind on preserving the species, and that settled it. As she willed, provision had to be made, so we captured a few calves and put them with milk cows," Charles recalled.[14] And according to Charles, "Mrs. Goodnight saved the buffalo for Texas."[15]

When E. J. Davison traveled to the Goodnight ranch to write a feature story for the *Ladies' Home Journal* in 1901, he described two square miles of pastureland covered with natural vegetation that had been fenced off for the buffalo. Some were purebred; others, a unique breed the Goodnights called "cataloes"—a buffalo and cow mix. Mary explained the distinction between purebred animals and the intriguing cataloes. Both displayed the signature hump and shaggy hair, but the cataloes had longer horns and more variety in the color of their coats. She said the cataloes could be trained to eat out of her hand, while the purebreds were much too shy and skittish. And she pointed out the two breeds self-segregated in the enclosure—the purebred looking "with a royal contempt upon his plebeian half-brother." Mary proudly showed Mr. Davison around the ranch. "We have about fifteen elks," she explained. "We have deer and antelopes. . . . Like the elks, the deer do not thrive well, and the antelopes generally die before they are a year old."[16]

While deer, elk, and antelope breeding turned out to be less successful for the Goodnights, Mary continued to protect her buffalo and expanded the purebred stock as well as the catalo herd. Her efforts to save the buffalo from extinction turned out to be an "immeasurable contribution to history."[17] She and Charles had started their buffalo herd in the spring of 1879 with a handful of young calves. In 1884, they began their experiment crossing Polled Angus and Galloway cattle with the buffalo. By 1888, they had 10 half-breed calves, and by 1894, Mary had 30 full-blood buffalo and about the same amount of mixed breed. In 1898, they had 45 purebred, and the number of crossbreds had grown to 60 with the birth of 15 calves that year. In 1907, 20 new calves were born, increasing the purebred herd to 80, in addition to 150 catalo on the ranch. In 1924, Charles told a reporter the ranch was home to 192 purebred buffalo.

In addition to breeding new stock, the Goodnights sold to zoos and circuses. In September 1899, the *Kansas City* (Missouri) *Journal* ran a story about Mary's business under the headline "Seven Buffalo Were Quite an Attraction Yesterday—Will Be Shipped to New York." The "shaggy,

Men skinning buffaloes, slaughtered for the hide. *Library of Congress Prints and Photographs Division, Washington, D.C.* Harper's Weekly, *1874 Dec. 12, v. 18, no. 937.* LC-USZ62-55602.

evil-looking" buffalo had just arrived from the Goodnight ranch in the "wild and woolly West."[18] The Greer-Mills Commission Company had consigned the creatures from the Goodnights, and famed buffalo-hunter-turned-breeder and friend of the Goodnights Charles Jesse "Buffalo" Jones had brought them from the Goodnight ranch, along with fifteen head of thoroughbred Polled Angus cattle, which Mary had bred and raised, according to the newspaper. The buffalo were headed to their new home at the New York Zoological Gardens in the Bronx, where they would be raised for breeding. The *New York Times* described the newly opened gardens as having attractive animal ranges, each surrounded by wire fencing, over acres of woods and meadows. Each range had a shelter house. The buffalo range was the largest situated in the southeast section of the park.

Accounts of the Goodnights' work to preserve and domesticate the buffalo have been told from different perspectives—some giving Charles sole credit, others claiming Mary was the driving force behind the enterprise. Charles himself had an opinion about Mary's role in their business. In a 1924 interview with Max Bentley with the *Fort Worth Star-Telegram* that focused primarily on *his* lifelong accomplishments (under the headline "Colonel Goodnight and Brave Wife"), Charles nodded in the direction of Mary, who sat silently by the fireside, and stated it was his wife who believed wholeheartedly in the possibility of domesticating buffalo, and it was her idea to perpetuate the bison species. At the same time, he seemed to take credit for the actual work: "I did it. In '78 I roped three heifers and a young bull and started breeding." He tempered his remarks by paying tribute to Mary as she sat listening. "She followed me into the wilderness, she drove the chuck wagon, lived in dugouts and missed the companionship, butter and eggs and things that women love. She roughed it with me through all the years, doing a drover's work. My wife has been a real companion," he added. The reporter closed his article by describing Mary's reaction: "Suddenly, Mrs. Goodnight roused herself. Turning to her husband's interviewer, she gave him an angelic smile, and, with an indescribably charming cadence in her voice, invited him to spend several days at the ranch."[19]

When writer Phebe K. Warner wrote about the Goodnights in 1919 and again in 1925, she didn't shy away from Mary's role in the history-making endeavor and concluded that together the Goodnights had embarked on "one of the most unique lessons in conservation that the State of Texas has ever known."[20] Mary's niece Annie Dyer Nunn, writing in 1931, gave recognition to a "lone woman" who, when "[p]ractically all that was left" of the wild buffalo was a "white sea of bleaching bones ... intervened to save the beginning of what is now probably the largest herd in America."[21]

Historical events and deeds attributed to individuals from the past are always open to interpretation. Absent Mary's voice—most of the interviews from the time came from Charles—Mary's role in the family business may be unclear. But some might interpret Mary's "angelic smile" and invitation to spend a few days at the Goodnight ranch as Mary's way of telling reporter Max Bentley to make his own judgments about who did the work associated with the Goodnights' buffalo enterprise.

Minna "Minnie" Eshleman Sherman

Society Girl Becomes Dairy Rancher

"We want strong cattle that are treated kindly enough from babyhood to think of the human family as friends, not as fiends."[1]

MINNIE ESHLEMAN SHERMAN, A CALIFORNIA BUSINESSWOMAN AND dairy cow expert, expressed her sentiments in her weekly column in the *California Cultivator* in 1899. Her reputation as a grape grower and dairy rancher was well established and in full view at her Minnewawa Dairy and Stock Farm located near Fresno. Minnie's barns reflected her belief that cows residing in clean, nurturing environments produced more and higher-quality milk than those raised in traditional settings. Her cement barn floors, plaster walls, and gutter system for carrying away manure were not typical at the time.[2]

Minna "Minnie" Eshleman Sherman. Saline *(MI)* Observer, *August 8, 1901.*

The "former society girl" label used by some to describe Minnie reflected on her early years in Philadelphia as a daughter of well-educated, wealthy parents.[3] Minnie graduated from an exclusive girls' school in Philadelphia and the University of Pennsylvania.

136

When her father, a medical doctor, suffered from health problems, the family moved to California, taking advantage of its mild climate. In 1886, twenty-something Minnie purchased the ranch she named Minnewawa and paid nearly $30,000 for the 480 acres. It's likely the money she used to buy the property was a gift from her father after the sale of a family mining venture.[4] That gift offered her an advantage in acquiring and developing a business opportunity, but it was her scientific approach to farming that many believed made her ranch, vineyard, and herd of Holstein dairy cows a splendidly successful venture. "I knew nothing of farming or country life. I had been trained for society," Minnie said years later. Yet within a few years of her land purchase, she had become known as the "most practical, scientific and successful woman farmer in California."[5]

When the Eshleman family arrived in California from Philadelphia, they had invested in mining operations, and Minnie, along with her father, honed her knowledge of business practices. But mining turned out to be a disappointment, and when Minnie acquired her share of the profits from the sale of the family mining enterprise, she invested in the land that became Minnewawa. It turned out to be a wise venture for a woman who at the age of ten, "all crisp and starchy" in her proper little dress and driven by the family coachman in a "one-horse brougham," had been entrusted to settle the weekly accounts with the grocer, fruit, and dry-goods dealers and deliver her father's earnings to the bank.[6]

Over the years, Minnie steadfastly experimented with and improved her methods for growing crops and raising dairy herds. "My land was unimproved with the exception of ten acres of wine-grapes," she said, "four acres of old vineyard of mixed varieties, and thirty acres of almonds."[7] She added another forty acres of muscat vines for raisin making, peaches, olives, and table grapes. Then she bought some registered Percheron horses and a herd of registered Holstein cattle.

Her innovative methods at first drew ridicule, but in time, it became apparent that Minnie's ideas, founded on scientific research and experimentation, were reliable and productive. She had always pruned her emperor table grapes close to the ground; when an Italian ranch hand advised pruning to four feet, she followed his lead, and the result was improved fruit bearers. She used dynamite to loosen the hard-packed

earth around her olive trees after carefully studying the soil and recall-
ing the practicality of dynamite at the family's mining operation. When
no one in the state was using silos to store food for ranch animals, she
built one of the first, filling it in the fall with green corn that was finely
chopped and mixed with dry feed to provide nutrition to the cows in the
dry months. She learned how to build her silo by reading about it in an
encyclopedia.

Cleanliness in her dairy was important to Minnie. She installed special folding stalls, making it easier to keep the area clean. She was determined to install cement floors in her dairy barn with drains that would
carry away manure. She and a dairy worker—on their knees as the cement
formed—used wine bottles to create the proper slope and curvature in the
wet cement to accommodate her unique methods. Unhappy to learn that
her packer cut the branches of her grapes to fit into his baskets, she built
a packing house on her ranch and used specially designed baskets to hold
the fruit without cutting the branches. As a special touch, she tied the
bunches of fruit together with ribbons. Her techniques brought a dollar a
crate more than those packed by her old packer. She also offered clusters
of grapes packed in elegant cartons to clients in New York for ten dollars
apiece.

Minnie's dairy herd and butter-making techniques became legendary and made her a sought-after speaker and writer in agricultural
circles. In 1900, she delivered a paper titled "Barn, Stalls, and Floors for
Cattle" at the seventh annual California Dairy Association convention.
In 1901, she spoke about "The Profitable Dairy Cow" at the Riverside
Farmers' Club Institute. In her article "Supplementing Alfalfa as Cow
Feed," she reminded readers that alfalfa was a heavy-protein food that
helped produce healthy cows and that "hearty eating and good digestion" were essential for high-milk-producing cows. Inadequate feeding
practices could result in "flighty, fidgety" cows—something no dairy
rancher wanted.[8] Minnie's cow named Lady Kathleen, a model for her
definition of a good cow, produced a record 629 pounds of butter in
1900. Another star producer in Minnie's herd was a cow named Juliana
de Kol, who had once produced just over twenty-five pounds of butter
in one week.

For Minnie, a carefully regimented recipe for feed made all the difference in high butter production. She used grain, coconut cake, bran, corn, and alfalfa and twice a week cooked oatmeal or linseed oil—a product she believed aided in the animal's digestion. And Lady Kathleen was a prime example. "Since I learned how to feed her this cow has never missed a meal," she said.[9]

Minnie carefully kept detailed records related to feed and milk production over the years. Those accounts guided her future practices. "Last year I found, after careful studying for five previous years' records, that to feed, milk and care for my cows was costing $51.06 per head," she said. "It then became apparent that no cow producing less than 300 pounds of butter was good for my use. . . . I am more and more convinced that cows that will not be thrifty under intelligent care are useless for the dairy."[10]

And when it came time to sell one of her cows or even the entire herd, her revenues were legendary. When other ranchers were getting twelve to fifteen dollars a head, Minnie sold hers for as much as sixty-five dollars. And her Holsteins went all over the world. She shipped seven to an English investor who was establishing a herd in Japan. She had plans to sell to Africa, but the deal fell through when the Boer War broke out. Closer to home, it was reported that she sold forty Holsteins to a Stockton, California, rancher for $10,000 in 1903.

She expanded her land holdings, buying up two smaller ranches and property in Fresno. At the peak of her ranching years, Minnie had more than one thousand acres in cultivation among her three ranches: Minnewawa, Palomitos Vineyard, and Keystone Ranch.[11] In September 1889, Minnie married Dr. W. N. Sherman, a "noble hearted, skillful surgeon" and "generous, sympathetic gentleman," according to one newspaper account.[12] He wholeheartedly leant his expertise to Minnie's ranching operations, taking special interest in the Percheron-horse-raising enterprise and the rabbitry division, developing a stock of Lord Banbury, Champion Yukon, and Lord Britain rabbit breeds. The doctor's "extensive and modern pens and hutches" were equipped to house up to three hundred rabbits.[13] He also delivered talks about the care of milk and the importance of cleanliness in dairy establishments, including the dangers of bacteria. He extolled the virtues of fruit growing in the Fresno area.

"Fresno is the geographical center of the State. Too many associate this section with dust and jack-rabbits. It is, however, one of the famous raisin growing centers of the world," he told the state's fruit growers at their convention in 1902.[14]

Minnie's ambitious spirit extended beyond her ranches as she became involved in community issues largely through her participation in various women's clubs, both locally and statewide.[15] Through these organizations, Minnie and the other members advocated for care of orphans, school accommodations for truants, nutrition classes and health care for women through the establishment of settlement organizations, day care for working mothers, and forestry conservation and beautification projects. She tackled tree planting in Fresno and the building of sidewalks and parks, and despite her love of dogs, she supported laws limiting free-running dogs, who trampled gardens and flowers.[16] In 1913 she became the second woman to be named a regent at the University of California.[17]

Minnie's passion for ranching never faded. "The zest is not gone, indeed, I am quite as keen as ever—that is, so long as I am trying new things," she said in a January 1913 interview. "You may laugh at this, but I shall plant plums because I have never had plums; and I shall plant Calimyrna figs, because I have never tried figs and this new variety is a wonder; and I want to try peaches again. . . . [S]o long as I am working with something new I am as keen as ever."[18] But Minnie had already accomplished some very impressive feats. According to the reporter who interviewed her, Minnie's approach to ranching as a science had "made all the gray-bearded ranchers in the state think they had better begin over and learn the a-b-c of ranching."[19]

Nancy B. Irving

Writer and Goat Rancher

"[T]he earth is big enough for us both and Colorado needs both the cattle and goat industries."[1]

NANCY B. IRVING IMPLORED CATTLE RANCHERS TO SUPPORT HER NEW goat-raising business in her adopted state in the summer of 1902. Days before, hundreds of goats had been slaughtered on her ranch near Grand Junction. She suspected the armed and masked marauders performed their unspeakable deeds at the direction of cattlemen in the area who resented the introduction of voracious goats to the precious grazing lands. While Nancy was new to the region, her reputation as a Chicago writer may have rankled some of the cattlemen. Her recently published book *Who Lies?* had attracted publicity for its claims that male business owners were incapable of telling the truth. She had offered $1,000 to the man who could prove that he did not lie in his professional and personal interactions. At the end of the contest, Nancy concluded that she could not find a man who measured up to her challenge. "A minister almost won the prize three months ago. But he lied in his eagerness to convince me that he did not lie," she said. "They all lost. Either they were honest and could not prove it, or they were dishonest and tired of trying to prove a lie."[2] So off to Colorado for city slicker Nancy—to start a goat ranch deep in the heart of cattle country, where most, if not all, of the ranchers were well-established businessmen.

Nancy had done her homework and was convinced a goat-raising endeavor would be a lucrative investment. "There ought to be money in

Advertisement for Nancy B. Irving's book *Who Lies?* Chicago Tribune, *June 9, 1901.*

goats," she said. "We will sell the wool, which will make mohair, and some of the goats will be sold as mutton." She claimed that goat meat was popular in France and England and could be in the United States. "There is a great market for it; we will sell considerably here," she said. She invested some of her own money and had lined up investors to form the Angora Ranch Association. Six of the investors were women; Nancy was president. "Everything we do has a risk in it; life is all only a game or gamble. I think I might as well try it; my friends had confidence enough in me to let me have their funds," she said.[3]

Nancy used the money to purchase land, construct buildings, and install an irrigation system. And most importantly, she put together a herd of beautiful Angora goats. She was aware of the cattlemen's opposition to sheep ranching in Colorado and knew her goats could pose a problem, too. Mindful of the situation, she intentionally bought land covered with "chico, rabbit-brush and low scrub-cedars . . . and scarcely a blade of grass"—favorable grazing munchies for goats but of little interest to cattle or their owners, she believed.[4] Before long, the kids were growing into chubby little rascals, and the mothers appeared to be thriving. There was an incident in early May, when a mountain lion or possibly a bobcat attacked the herd. For several nights, Nancy had heard animal noises, but in the morning light, there was no evidence that any of the goats had been harmed. One night, though, the goats suffered a deadly attack. A kid and its mother were victims. The kid was almost entirely eaten by a "voracious beast," and the mother "had tender parts eaten away," according to the newspaper. Nancy asked local youth to organize a hunting party to "exterminate these beasts" who had killed her goats. She swore to launch a "vigorous campaign against the foe."[5] She couldn't have known at the time that she and her goats were soon to encounter a much more voracious beast—insatiable humans unwilling to share resources.

MRS. NANCY B. IRVING,
The Colorado Woman Who Has Gained Admiration by Spiritedly Defending Her Angora Goat Ranch Against Organized Raiders.

Nancy B. Irving, goat rancher. St. Louis (MO) Globe-Democrat, August 5, 1902, in Newspapers.com.

On the evening of July 26, Nancy's herder, Lloyd Kellogg, was sitting down to eat supper with a couple of friends at a camp on the ranch when three men wearing black masks entered their cabin with drawn revolvers and demanded, "Throw up your hands!" The startled herders thought the visitors were playing a joke but soon learned the intruders were deadly serious. "[W]hen they pushed a rifle into my face, they said they were in earnest and I put them up," Lloyd said. They ordered the herders to face the wall while they bound the men. A short time later, the masked men returned to the cabin and told Lloyd to notify his employer that she needed to leave with her goats or expect a return visit. "They told us on penalty of death not to stick our heads out of the cabin that night. . . . They locked the doors when they went away," Lloyd said, "and when they said we should not stick our head out of the window we took them at their word." The next morning, when Lloyd made his way to the corral where the goats had been enclosed for the evening, he found a horrendous sight.

Hundreds of goats and kids had been clubbed and axed. Many were dead, but some were badly injured, crying in agony. Lloyd said the moans from the injured animals were "almost human."[6] He faced the sickening task of putting the poor creatures out of their misery.

Local law enforcement was notified of the slaughter and arrived at the scene. Sheriff William Struthers could find no trace of the culprits and posted some of his deputies at the ranch to protect the remainder of the goats. Nancy went to the office of the *Daily Sentinel* newspaper in Grand Junction and gave her version of the tragedy. Estimating her loss at $6,000, she said she had notified the governor. "I desire to see if the moral sentiment of the state of Colorado and the people of this city and county will tolerate such a high-handed outrage," she said. "The goats at the time they were killed were not trespassing on the property of anyone."[7] A Salt Lake City newspaper in reporting the incident insisted that Nancy would "have the sympathy of the entire community" in her loss.[8] Nancy appealed to her fellow ranchers in a letter in the *Daily Sentinel* addressed to the "Cattlemen's Association of Mesa County": "I have been told that your organization is responsible for the killing of my Angora goats. I don't believe it. I don't think that such men as I know many cattlemen to be would countenance such a deed." She added, "We are both factors in the development of the resources of Colorado, each is needed, and goats don't eat grass."[9]

Over the next weeks, as no arrests were made and her situation gained little attention, Nancy was outspoken about the economic value of goat ranching compared to raising cattle in Colorado. "A cattle outfit will run a herd over a certain territory until its range resources are exhausted, and then it is shifted, leaving the agricultural and business community no better off for their presence," she said. "The number of men employed is small as compared to the number required to handle Angoras. The Angora industry requires permanent quarters and two fixed camps, one on the summer and the other on the winter range. During lambing and shearing seasons, the working force must be greatly augmented, giving employment to the citizens of the immediate community." She added, "It seems to me the contrast makes the benefits of the Angora business to the community obvious."[10] She announced that she had been in negotiations with Chicago businessman Aaron Montgomery Ward, founder of Montgomery Ward and Company, to establish a factory at Grand Junction that would treat the mohair from her goats and prepare it for market.

However, by the fall of 1902, Nancy had begun to show signs of defeat. A Denver women's club declined her offer to speak to the group about her experiences because the "club did not wish to listen to female politicians."[11] She had gotten little or no response from groups and individuals to whom she had appealed. One sympathizer summarized Nancy's situation, saying, "All of officialdom was palsied in the face of this atrocious crime." He described how her petition to the governor was "summarily dismissed," lawyers were "sensibly discreet," the legislature had "kept silence," and the courts "have shown no 'welcome' over their doors."[12] And when Nancy approached the Board of County Commissioners, they failed to act. Two of the three members were cattle ranchers, and the third had been accused of participating in a sheep slaying some years earlier. "It was as if you came to me for help when someone was burning down your house, and I wouldn't even go to see, but just stood around in idle gossip and did nothing but talk about you," Nancy said.[13]

In October, she sent letters to her investors stating that "it would be useless to continue struggling against the warfare waged by the cattlemen."[14] She had surrendered to the cattlemen and would be moving the goats out of Colorado. She was considering starting a goat ranch near Cuba, Missouri, where she had shipped about four hundred of her remaining Colorado herd to live temporarily. Some Missouri farmers had bought some of her herd to clear off brush. "Southwest Missouri, I understand, extends excellent advantages for my business," she said.[15]

It's unclear that Nancy ever started her goat ranch in Missouri, but she did cause a sensation again in 1904, when David A. Smith, a clerk in the county court of Salt Lake City, told a newspaper reporter that his "breath almost left him" when a couple came to his office for a marriage license on August 19. The young man gave his age as twenty-three, and the woman was "old enough to be his mother." He could find no reason to deny the couple their wish and granted a license to Elzie C. Miller and Nancy B. Irving. After issuing the couple their license and performing the marriage ceremony with Helena A. McIntosh and Cora S. Dixon as witnesses, Mr. Smith, who also happened to be an elder in the Church of Jesus Christ of Latter-Day Saints, reported he "sent the woman on her way rejoicing with her young husband."[16]

Part IX

Livestock Traders

"[I]t is half-past five o'clock ... the stock loudly pleading to be turned into the pastures.... I now drive the two cows, a half-quarter mile and turn them in with the others, come back, and then there's a horse in the barn that belongs in a field where there is no water, which I take to a spring quite a distance from the barn; bring it back and turn it into a field with the sheep.... The young calves are then turned out into the warm sunshine, and the stock hogs ... are clamoring for feed, and I carry a pailful of swill to them, and hasten to the house and turn out the chickens and put out feed and water for them.... I have not eaten breakfast yet, but that can wait; I make the beds next and straighten things up in the living room, for I dislike to have the early morning caller find my house topsy-turvy."[1]

Elizabeth Smith Collins

Taking Her Cattle to the Stockyards

"[T]HE COMMISSION MEN SAY SHE IS WELL ABLE TO TAKE CARE OF HER interests" and that she "secured prices which testify to a woman's ability at bargaining." High praise for any cattle rancher and remarkable for a *woman* at Chicago's Union Stock Yards in 1895. Elizabeth Smith Collins, or Libby, as she was commonly known, had established a reputation as a shrewd negotiator and "remarkable financier" who was "equally ready to crack a joke or drive a hard bargain."[1]

Her journey to the rough-and-tumble world of the Chicago yards had started when as a young girl she traveled in a covered wagon with her family from Illinois and Iowa across the plains to Denver in 1855. Her dad was chasing his dreams of pulling gold from the Colorado earth, only to die before making his fortune. Her mother, a brother, and Libby were left to carry on, tackling each setback with relentless spirit. Denver at the time presented a danger with its rowdy reputation as a tough frontier town. As she walked along a main street past a gambling tent one day, a stray bullet struck Libby just above her knee, and although only a slight wound, the healing process was "not of a very pleasant nature."[2]

When her brother returned from a prospecting trip with severely frozen hands, face, and feet at the same time her mother suffered from erysipelas, a severe skin infection, Libby took on the care of two motherless children. And when Libby was captured and held prisoner by a band of Indians, the family endured a time of uncertainty and anxiety. But upon her rescue, Libby and her brother were fortunate to obtain jobs on a wagon train traveling from Colorado east to the Missouri River. As cook for 160 hungry men, seventeen-year-old Libby, the only female on the train, had her hands full. Over the next two years, Libby made a dozen trips with the wagon train. Each was filled with its trials but also was a learning experience for Libby. There were the summer sandstorms, dirt and sand "cutting a person's face, filling his mouth, nose, ears, and eyes," and the winter storms when Libby awoke "to find the blankets which covered me weighted down with a layer of snow from two to four inches thick."[3]

By the ripe old age of nineteen, Libby was ready for a change and made her way to Virginia City, Montana, a mining town with job opportunities for her and her brother. Libby found work cleaning and cooking for miners and rented a sewing machine for seven dollars a month so she could work as a seamstress. Over the next few years, she moved from one mining camp to another, working as a cook and also picking up some skills as a nurse, working for a time for a doctor. It was also at a mining camp that Libby met a mine owner named Nat Collins, who became her husband in 1874.

As a wedding gift, Nat had given his bride a cow, and although it was a hefty investment of seventy-five dollars, that cow would become the start of a very lucrative enterprise for the couple. Within a few years, the Collins decided to sell their mining business and rented a ranch to raise what had become a herd of 180 cattle in the Prickly Pear Valley. After a particularly severe winter, they looked to moving to the Teton Valley, where they bought a ranch near the settlement called Old Agency, later known as Choteau, and tended their herd of cattle carrying their unique brand, "77." Because the ranch was rich with "swift-running streams" and "verdant foothills" to offer shelter to their stock in extreme weather, their herd grew to thousands.[4] In 1886, they made their last move, this time to Willow Creek, about twenty-four miles from Choteau.

Being a "woman richly endowed with Western pluck and enterprise," Libby was an integral part of the cattle business from the beginning. "She could ride a horse or use a rifle or pistol as well as any man," according to newspaper reports. And as the Collins' cattle enterprise grew, Libby's role in the business drew attention. "No one knows what it means to ride days and nights with a through cattle train except those who have had to do it," a New York reporter wrote in 1894. And Libby was someone who knew the experience because she "accompani[ed] her stock and [saw] that they [had] proper treatment in their long journey across four States."[5]

As their herd had grown to thousands, Libby and Nat had joined other ranchers in selling their cattle to livestock buyers who had come to the ranches offering prices that the ranchers haggled over but ultimately accepted. It was in 1889 that Libby began to rethink their traditional way of doing business when it was time to sell some of their cattle. Libby, who by some accounts was the "brains, energy and push" behind the ranching operation, questioned the wisdom of dealing with a buyer.[6] Why not bypass him and go directly to the stockyards with the cattle? Surely, she could secure a better profit by eliminating the middleman. So Libby set out on the first leg of the trip from the Collins ranch in 1891, driving a bunch of cattle with some faithful cowboys from the ranch to Great Falls to catch a train that would transport the cattle to Chicago's Union Stock Yards.

"For a woman to undertake such a task and carry it through to a successful ending was an event as yet unheard of in the history of the cattle trade.... I determined to try.... [W]hen the time had come for the start, it found me ready, dressed and prepared to mount the 'grub wagon,'" Libby recalled years later.[7] The four-day journey from the ranch to Great Falls was uneventful. Camping out each night, Libby and the cowboy drovers arrived in Great Falls ready to load the cattle onto the stock train cars, which Libby had lined up for the trip to Chicago. But she met resistance when she arrived. The railroad company wanted a full train of twenty-two cars with each car containing twenty-two cattle before it would take off for the city. It was an annoying delay, but before long, drovers from other ranches arrived with cattle to fill out the train cars. The other challenge Libby faced was not as easily surmounted. It was customary for the rail company to grant free tickets to shippers so they could travel to Chicago with their animals. They rode in the caboose, fitted out with wooden benches along the sides of the car. It's possible some of the cabooses were neat, clean, far from luxurious, yet comfortable enough, but typically, they were not. Cabooses, only about nine feet in width and with benches eating up additional precious space, didn't leave much leg room for riders. The constant deafening clang of the wheels, cigar and cigarette smoke clinging to the stagnant air, and wads of juicy chewing tobacco sprinkled over the floor combined with whiskey-slugging, poker-playing cattlemen often made the trip an interesting journey. Apparently, at least some railroad companies believed livestock trains were not fit for female habitation.

"Among the rules of the railroad company, I was informed, was one which prohibited the granting of a pass to a lady who wished to accompany stock upon a cattle train," Libby said. "I vowed to secure my rights and accompany my stock to market."[8] Hitching a team of horses to a wagon at the campsite where she and the cowboys waited for the second leg of the trip, Libby requested a meeting with a representative of the livestock firm that had purchased her cattle. She was determined to "ascertain why [she] should be denied" the privilege of riding with her cattle on the train.[9] She asked the fellow to telegraph railroad officials headquartered in St. Paul, Minnesota, and obtain permission for her to ride the train with her cattle. Very shortly after her meeting, the local railroad agent provided Libby with a pass ensuring railroad employees "treat her with all respect due a lady." When the day came for Libby and her cattle to board the train to Chicago, she climbed the steps to the "smoke-stained caboose" and turned toward the platform to find a crowd of cowboys and ranchers raising their hats in the air and chanting, "Success to Aunty Collins, the Cattle Queen of Montana."[10]

When Libby arrived in St. Paul, railroad officials greeted her at a local hotel, handing over first-class tickets for the remainder of her trip to Chicago and allowing her to arrive in advance of her cattle. When she reached the Windy City, she headed to the stockyards to pick up her payment for the cattle, delighted to realize the amount was several hundred dollars more than she had been offered back at the ranch by a cattle buyer. It confirmed for Libby that bypassing the traveling livestock buyers who came to the ranches was the best decision she had made and the best course in the future.

Libby continued to travel with her cattle to the Chicago market over the years. However, as Libby noted, during her early years on the ranch her actions "occasioned much comment on the part of the newspapers and magazines throughout the country." According to one account, Libby was the "first and only lady in Montana to raise, ship and accompany the train bearing her stock to the Chicago market." And furthermore, she "personally superintend(s) the unloading of the animals and their sale." Other ranchers turned to Libby for her expertise. "She is well informed on every subject pertaining to stock raising, and her judgment is often asked by others regarding purchases and other matters pertaining to the industry," a newspaper article reported about the "Cattle Queen of Montana."[11]

Her appearance at the stockyards became commonplace, and she became a bit of a celebrity. "She is neither a new woman nor typical of the wild west, but a big woman, motherly looking and kind hearted," according to a news article in 1895. Being large in stature, Libby's weight was sometimes a topic of speculation in news articles. And her clothing became newsworthy as this highly successful businesswoman negotiated returns on her investments. "She wore a shiny black shirt waist with mother-of-pearl cuff buttons, a black belt, and changeable tie knotted in jaunty fashion. Instead of the traditional sailor hat a black open straw bonnet with nodding sprays of minionette," a Kansas newspaper reported during one of Libby's business trips to Chicago.[12]

Libby's cattle-raising days were a lucrative endeavor and one that she enjoyed. However, she had always had a vivid interest in mining, stemming from her time working in mining camps, and in 1897, a news article indicated that Libby was involved in a mine in Columbia Falls, Montana, where she had been "giving her personal attention to the workings of the mine." Libby was quoted by the newspaper: "I know a great deal about mining, miners and mines. . . . [M]any a hardy miner has asked me to examine his 'prospect' and tell him what I thought of it."[13] It may have been her lifelong fascination with mines or memories of her dad's quest for gold in her childhood, but at one time during her ranching days, the gold bug bit Libby. "I was tiring of the quiet life I was forced to lead," she said. And when talk of gold in Alaska reached the Montana ranch, Libby's interest was piqued. "I felt the desire for excitement burn in my blood and could not resist," she said.[14] She set out for Alaska. "There was gold there—plenty of it; we could see it in the sand, even in the grass roots; but there was no water with which to pan it out. It was tantalizing to know

The Chicago Stockyards about the time Elizabeth Smith Collins took her cattle there. *Library of Congress, LC-USZ62-49270.*

MRS. NAT. COLLINS

The Cattle Queen of Montana.
In her Celebrated Illustrated Entertainments

"WANDERINGS IN THE WEST"

An Interesting Recital of Personal Experience of more
than Forty Years in the Far West, Elaborately Illustrated by over 300 Special Colored Views.

"FROM THE GREAT MISSOURI
TO THE DOME OF THE ROCKIES"

Across the Plains, Through the Mountains and
Over the Glaciers.

Broadside of Mrs. Nat Collins lecture tour. *Catalog # P-760, Montana Historical Society Research Center Photograph Archives, Helena, Montana.*

that a fortune lay at our feet, but we lacked the means of securing it," Libby said.[15] So failing to make a fortune in gold, she returned to her Montana ranch. Three years after her return from Alaska, Nat died.

Libby had led a fascinating life, and when she wrote her autobiography, *The Cattle Queen of Montana*, it was a hit, which led to her next big adventure—delivering lectures about her ventures from the time of her youth in the Midwest to her ranching days.[16] Her publisher, C. W. Foote, acted as her advance man and manager, and she traveled around Montana as well as to other states with her talk titled "Wanderings in the West." It was billed as "An Interesting Recital of Personal Experience of More Than Forty Years in the Far West."

Libby's compelling life experiences captured the attention of many during her lifetime. Her lectures and autobiography provided glimpses into her personality and explained the allure of this Montana pioneer. She welcomed visitors to her ranch "[d]ay or night, rain or shine, storm or calm." And she promised strangers and friends alike would be "met a hearty, cordial and sincere welcome," so long as "there remains upon the range a single hoof bearing the 77 brand."[17] As for that title "Cattle Queen of Montana": "[I]n its possession I experience much pride," Libby said.[18] "I would rather to-day be the 'Cattle Queen' of the Montana cowboys than sit upon the throne of Queen Victoria."[19]

Jennie M. Goodwin

Livestock Commission Merchant

"I want to be my own boss, for I am capable of managing my affairs according to my own ideas."[1]

TWENTY-FOUR-YEAR-OLD JENNIE GOODWIN, BY MOST ACCOUNTS THE first female livestock commission merchant in Kansas City, had just opened her tastefully furnished office and was eager to welcome her first customers in the summer of 1895. The official definition of a livestock commission merchant fit Jennie perfectly: "one who receives, sells, or buys livestock and charges a commission for the same."[2]

She'd been working in the livestock business in the city for about seven years by this time. After completing a course at a business college, she had landed a job as a stenographer in the offices of the American Livestock Company, a commission firm that eventually fell into disfavor with cattlemen and ended up defending itself in court. Despite the company's questionable reputation, Jennie had won the admiration of livestock ranchers and shippers throughout the region, earning the affectionate title the "American Girl."[3] And when the firm went out of business, she moved on to another livestock commission firm, the Campbell Live Stock Commission, where she was a stenographer and took on some accounting duties, as well. But that firm also went out of business. It was a pivotal time for Jennie.

"I was very tired the evening the Campbell company went out of business," Jennie said. "I had just finished a hard day's work on the typewriter

Jennie Goodwin. Our Mountain Home *(Talladega, Alabama), October 9, 1895.*

and felt there was no future in that line of work. I wanted to do something on a larger scale. The idea occurred to me to go into the live stock business for myself."[4]

And so, with a loyal network of potential customers in place, office space rented, years of experience under her belt, and a determined mindset, Jennie embarked on her venture. But was the all-male Kansas City livestock enclave willing to open its arms to a woman attempting to break barriers? It became a dilemma for the powerful Kansas City Live Stock Exchange, an organization set up to "promote and protect all interests connected with the buying and selling of live stock."[5] Comprised of owners of large and small livestock commission firms and representatives from the local packing plant and the Kansas City Stockyards Company, the exchange was formed in 1886, operating under a constitution, bylaws, and a board of directors. With hundreds of livestock commission merchants operating in Kansas City and thousands of cattle, sheep, and hogs streaming into the stockyards each day, there was a need for overall coordination of processes, transportation, animal housing, and communication. The exchange fulfilled many of those duties—from overseeing the flow of paperwork between buyers and sellers and arranging the schedules of stock trains arriving and departing Kansas City to lobbying for livestock interests in Washington and communicating daily market quotes from such major markets as Chicago and Omaha.[6] Belonging to the Kansas City Live Stock Exchange offered commission merchants definite advantages in operating their business.

According to a local newspaper, for commission merchants, membership in the exchange was "necessary to do business."[7] However, from its inception in 1886 until 1895, when Jennie established her business, no women were "mentioned in the Exchange records," nor was there evidence of Black or Latino/Latina members in those early years.[8] Jennie's membership in the exclusive club was to become a sticking point. Meanwhile, Jennie had a business to run, and customers were lining up.

The minute Texas "cattle king and multi-millionaire" Abel Head "Shanghai" Pierce heard Jennie had opened her livestock commission firm, he let it be known he intended to be a customer.[9] The six-foot-five rancher had brought thousands of cattle up to Kansas City over the years and knew Jennie from her days at the American Livestock Company and the Campbell firm. And he had great respect for her.

On his first visit to the city after Jennie opened Goodwin Commission Company, Shanghai declared his commitment: "I'll be the first on the ground, even if the cattle market is a little dull. She's the first girl who ever tried her hand in the live stock commission business, and we are going to see her through," Shanghai said. "She knows more than many of the men, and understands the business."[10] He wired a foreman back at his ranch in Texas, instructing him to send three carloads of his fat steers up to Kansas City. It was Jennie's first consignment, and by the end of the day, she had sold all seventy-two cattle at an average of $2.80 per hundred pounds. Her commission was $36.

Jennie had hired a stenographer and two seasoned salesmen: Harry M. Benham for hogs and Henry George, an old-time cattle salesman who had been dealing since 1872, about the year Jennie was born. And she intentionally sought out a male for the stenographer position. "I can get much more work out of a man than I could out of three women. It takes a man to manage a woman, and vice versa," she said. And while Jennie's personal office was a clean, tidy space for business transactions, she also offered her "cowhide booted cattle punching customers" an outside area where they could "lounge and expectorate and smoke their stockyard cigars without damage to either her furniture or her feelings."[11] But Jennie was less concerned with her office furnishings than with her efforts to establish a successful business. "[A]ll I want is a fair share of the business.

My six years' experience has taught me many things and I have seen others make enough mistakes to profit by them," she said.[12]

One aspect of the livestock business that Jennie rejected was the use of solicitors, individuals who worked for commission merchant firms to develop relationships with ranchers and encourage them to consign their stock to specific commission houses.[13] The practice became controversial when some solicitors used unscrupulous methods, such as offering bribes to ranchers in exchange for promises to consign with a firm. Competition for the ranchers' business was fierce, and it wasn't unusual for fights to break out among solicitors in the Kansas City stockyards. Jennie wanted no part of this unsavory activity. "I will have no solicitors, but have considerable business already promised to me," she said. Jennie believed honest commission merchants who offered good service did not have to resort to underhanded practices. "[S]hippers are not under obligations to consign to certain commission houses, and through the competition for business that will follow the shipper is assured the best of service, and the commission man who merits it will control the volume of patronage," she said.[14]

And Jennie's predictions seemed to prove true as her firm became established. Her first customer, "Shanghai" Pierce, appreciated the return he had gotten from her favorable service, and others followed. John Kirchenschlager, another livestock man in the area, put his faith in Jennie's reputation and fair-minded business practices, selling her sixty-one hogs that he had raised from piglets. These little "beauties" averaged 345 pounds and brought John just over $3.67 per hundred pounds.[15] He was very pleased with his earnings, and Jennie was proud, as her firm "topped the market" that day.[16]

Jennie had been involved in the livestock business as an employee of other livestock firms for years and understood the market as well as anyone. She planned to operate her business "on an economical basis." She considered the current financial climate from the perspective of her potential customers. "Everything looks favorable to the shipper. Money is easy and crops good. The feeders are able to borrow money on their cattle from their home banks at a less rate than commission firms can supply them. Confidence has been restored and country banks are willing to lend money with cattle as security," she observed. It was reported that other entrepreneurs recognized Jennie's business acumen and offered to partner with her, but she rejected their offers. "I want to be my own boss," she said.[17] She explained, "I find that it is not a complicated or difficult matter to manage a commission house. On myself alone rests the entire responsibility."[18] And Jennie was aware that she would have advantages if she joined the exchange; so, soon after opening her new office, she applied for membership in the group. It was expected that by the time her application was approved, she would pay the $1,000 membership fee.

The Kansas City Live Stock Exchange board of directors typically met twelve times a year, and in September 1895, they considered Jennie's membership application, approving it "[b]y eight yea votes."[19] It's unclear why Jennie failed to follow through with the process, but at the November meeting of the exchange, the board of directors again discussed Jennie's application, invited her to attend a meeting, and asked her to "show cause for not securing a membership in the Exchange." They gave her a deadline of January 1896 "to take out a certificate of membership in this Exchange."[20] A cadre of thirteen members called for a meeting on December 19 to discuss the "advisability of giving Miss Jennie Goodwin

Kansas City Live Stock Exchange Building. *Kansas City (MO) Public Library.*

a certificate of membership in the Exchange." This action would relieve Jennie of the burden of paying the $1,000 fee. However, at the meeting, a letter was read "in which Miss Jennie Goodwin stated that she did not desire the Members to make a precedent of giving her a membership in the Exchange."[21] Shortly after, Jennie's business closed its doors.

Local newspapers gave conflicting accounts of Jennie's situation. Some reported the high membership fee had made it impossible for Jennie to join the exchange, and it was nearly impossible to do business as a commission firm without exchange membership. The *Kansas City Star* reported that it was simply a temporary situation and that she closed "because of the bad condition of the stock business which this time of the year always brings on." She said her business had been brisk "while range cattle were coming in" and that she intended to reopen in the spring. "I will have no trouble in getting back all of my old customers then if I decide to resume," she said. Meanwhile, she planned to retain her office and provide a typewriting service to other commission firms. She added that her business had suffered from the dirty tricks instigated by some of the solicitors operating in the area. "[O]ne solicitor, just because I would not employ him ... went out into the country and worked to get one of my customers. When he failed to get him he asked him to send his stock to anybody else but me." She added, "I don't think any woman should try to go into active competition with men. The women are too good to succeed. The men work tricks so dirty that a woman does not even think of them."[22]

In 1897, the federal government brought a suit against the Kansas City Live Stock Exchange, accusing it of "monopolizing the business of buying and selling live stock at the Kansas City yards," partly because of their rule that "prohibited all dealings between members of the association and non-members."[23] Jennie was one of several commission merchants who submitted sworn depositions in support of the government prosecutors. She alleged that when she started her commission firm, she was "awaited upon by members of the exchange and notified to become a member," and when she refused, the exchange "notified her the time had expired," and she said she was "finally driven out of business by the exchange."[24]

It's unclear that Jennie ever reopened her livestock commission firm. She drew attention in the fall of 1896, when she rode in the annual horse show in Kansas City using a man's saddle and wearing a divided skirt. In 1899, she was working as stenographer for the livestock agent at the Santa Fe Railway Company and was described by a trade publication, the *Live Stock Inspector*, as the "Queen of the Kansas City Stock Yards" and the "most popular lady connected with this big and growing market."[25]

Conclusion

THE ANONYMOUS WOMAN WHO CONTRIBUTED THE CHAPTER TITLED "The Life Story of a Farmer's Wife" in the book *The Life Stories of Undistinguished Americans as Told by Themselves* in 1906 yearned for a life far from her Illinois farm, where an unappreciative husband and soul-crippling day-to-day responsibilities quashed her literary dreams. For her, joining with her husband in a farming operation offered little in the way of pleasure. Feelings of inadequacy, isolation, inferiority, and hopelessness smothered any sparks of contentment. By her own admission, she was miserably unsuited for the life of a grower, herder, tender of livestock, and housekeeper—impractical in ways that exasperated her wholly practical husband and baffled friends.

If she had interacted with the women of *Grit, Not Glamour*—who, for the most part, pursued and embraced their situations—what thoughts might have filled her head? Would she have been touched yet a little envious of the close relationship, bolstered with mutual love and respect, of 80 John and Laura Owen Wallace on their Texas ranch? Would she have empathized with Minnie Eshleman Sherman, who delighted in the marvels of dairy science at her California operation? Would the lawless antics and notoriety of Emma Watson incite just a trickle of intrigue for the nameless Illinois woman? Almost certainly, the writing careers of Belle von Dorn Harbert, Midy Morgan, and Kate Field would have turned her green with envy.

It seems fitting to end with a few lines from a poem by Popsie McIntosh, the "cowgirl of the Panhandle," who successfully melded her literary skills with her duties on the family ranch in Texas. Composed on the range as she herded cattle in 1887, "The Texican Steer" appeared in newspapers across the country and delighted members of the Lost Creek Literary Club in Arizona at their inaugural meeting. As she took to the stage "with the aromatic odor of the Texas steer" clinging to her skirts— "figuratively speakin'"—Popsie warned the audience that her literary work "may be lacking in poetic glare; it may display no grand pyrotechnic fervor; it may not flow along with any great degree of rhythmical glide." Still, the audience responded at the end of the recitation with "almost deafening" applause and twice called Popsie back to the stage to "bow her acknowledgments of the compliment."[1]

An excerpt from Popsie McIntosh's poem "The Texican Steer":

I once roped a beautiful steer, but I fell;
Fell from my pony with ear-piercing yell;
Fell with the lariat fast to my wrist;
Fell to be dragged through the grass wet with mist.
Bumping,
Rolling,
Screaming I went,
A full mile a minute or I don't want a cent.
The gravel and grass yanked the hide from my nose,
And ruined a new pair of forty-cent hose—
Aye, even my back hair was thrown out of gear
By the frolicsome freaks of that beautiful steer.

Notes

Introduction

1. "The Life Story of a Farmer's Wife," in *The Life Stories of Undistinguished Americans as Told by Themselves*, ed. Hamilton Holt (New York: James Pott, 1906), 150–66.

Part I

1. "The Life Story of a Farmer's Wife," in *The Life Stories of Undistinguished Americans as Told by Themselves*, ed. Hamilton Holt (New York: James Pott, 1906), 152.

Chapter 1

1. Hettye Wallace Branch, *The Story of 80 John: A Biography of One of the Most Respected Negro Ranchmen in the Old West* (New York: Greenwich Book, 1960), 40.

2. Hertha Auburn Webb, "D. W. '80 John' Wallace: Black Cattleman 1875–1939" (master's thesis, Prairie View Agricultural and Mechanical College, August 1957), 17.

3. Webb, "D. W. '80 John' Wallace," 23.

4. Wallace Branch, *Story of 80 John*, 30.

5. Webb, "D. W. '80 John' Wallace," 27.

6. Wallace Branch, *Story of 80 John*, 39.

7. Webb, "D. W. '80 John' Wallace," 33.

8. Wallace Branch, *Story of 80 John*, 39.

9. Wallace Branch, *Story of 80 John*, 40.

10. "'80-John' Left True West Texas Ranching Legacy," *Odessa* (Texas) *American*, April 30, 1995.

11. "Golden Wedding Celebration for Midland Negroes," *Abilene* (Texas) *Reporter News*, April 20, 1938.

12. "'80-John' Left True West."

13. Al McMichael, phone interview, March 9, 2021.

14. Mrs. C. C. Hamilton, "Aged Negress Has Lived Area History," *Abilene* (Texas) *Reporter-News*, June 4, 1950.

15. Wallace Branch, *Story of 80 John*, 41.

16. Wallace Branch, *Story of 80 John*, 51.

17. Find a Grave, n.d., findagrave.com/memorial/38217523/laura-dee-wallace#view-photo=48677628.

Chapter 2

1. Kitty Barry, "Woman Runs Farm in Summer; Travels over World in Winter," *Fort Worth Star-Telegram*, January 26, 1913.

2. "Missouri Woman a Great Traveler," *Calgary* (Canada) *Herald*, April 15, 1911.

3. Barry, "Woman Runs Farm."

4. "She Is Farmer, Club Woman and Traveler," *Evening Missourian*, March 19, 1911.

5. "Women's News," *Pittston* (Pennsylvania) *Gazette*, July 29, 1911.

6. "Missouri Woman a Great Traveler."

7. Barry, "Woman Runs Farm."

8. "Women's News."

9. "Women's News."

10. Rebecca S. Montgomery, "With the Brain of a Man and the Heart of a Woman: Missouri Women and Rural Change, 1890–1915," *Missouri Historical Review* (April 2010): 174.

11. Montgomery, "With the Brain of a Man."

12. Frances Pearle Mitchell, "President's Address," in *Missouri Agricultural Report: Forty-Fourth Annual Report of the Missouri State Board of Agriculture: A Record of the Work for the Year 1911* (Jefferson City, MO: Hugh Stephens, 1912), 293.

13. Mitchell, "President's Address," 292.

14. Charles B. Warren, "Address of Welcome," in *Proceedings of Third American Road Congress* (Baltimore, MD: Waverly Press, 1914), 8.

15. See Sam Pollard, dir., *Slavery by Another Name* (PBS, 2012), pbs.org/show/slavery-another-name/; and Ellen Terrell, "The Convict Leasing System: Slavery in Its Worst Aspects," *Inside Adams* (blog), June 17, 2021, blogs.loc.gov/inside_adams/2021/06/convict-leasing-system/.

16. "Women's Conference on Roads," in *Proceedings of the Fourth American Road Congress* (Baltimore, MD: Waverly Press, 1915), 343.

17. "Women's Conference on Roads," 343.

18. "Women's Conference on Roads," 344.

19. "Women's Conference on Roads," 345.

20. "Urges Back to Land Movement," *Los Angeles Express*, March 16, 1914.

21. "Missouri Woman a Great Traveler."

22. "About Woman's Opportunity as a Practical Farmer," *Cordell* (Oklahoma) *Beacon*, July 30, 1914.

Part II

1. "The Life Story of a Farmer's Wife," in *The Life Stories of Undistinguished Americans as Told by Themselves*, ed. Hamilton Holt (New York: James Pott, 1906), 165–66.

Chapter 3

1. "The Tyrant Man Says, No Trousers for Women," *San Francisco Examiner*, February 6, 1900.

2. "Girls Who Run Cattle Ranches," *Buffalo* (NY) *Evening News*, June 27, 1900.

3. "A Girl Who Runs a Ranch," *Butte* (MT) *Miner*, February 25, 1900.

4. "Girl Who Runs a Ranch."

5. "Girl Who Runs a Ranch."

6. "Girl Who Runs a Ranch."

7. "Girl Who Runs a Ranch."

8. "Girls Who Run Cattle Ranches."

9. "Two Modest Dianas of Mendocino County," *San Francisco Call*, October 31, 1897.

10. "Girl Who Runs a Ranch."

11. "Girl Who Runs a Ranch."

12. "Girl Who Runs a Ranch."

13. "Girl Who Runs a Ranch."

14. "Girl Who Runs a Ranch."

15. "Girl Who Runs a Ranch."

16. "Tyrant Man Says."

17. "Tyrant Man Says."

Chapter 4

1. "Seven Girls Who Own and Operate a 725 Acre Ranch," *Chicago Tribune*, October 16, 1904.

2. "Seven Girls." The headline mentions seven women, while the reporter describes eight in the body of the article. Many news accounts and photos at the time provided conflicting numbers. However, there were eight Vidal sisters who owned and operated the family ranch.

3. "Salida News," *Whitehorn News*, May 31, 1901.

4. "Girls Run a Ranch," *Watertown* (WI) *News*, November 23, 1904.

5. "Regis Vidal," Gunnison County, Colorado Genealogy and History, genealogytrails.com/colo/gunnison/bios2.html.

6. "New Ways for Girls to Make Money," *San Francisco Examiner*, October 23, 1904.

7. "New Ways."

8. "At the Lyric," *Wichita* (KS) *Eagle*, January 29, 1905.

9. William Jones, "Harry Buckwalter: Pioneer Colorado Filmmaker," *Film History* 4, no. 2 (1990): 89–100, jstor.org/stable/3814994.

10. "Seven Girls."

11. "New Ways."

Part III

1. "The Life Story of a Farmer's Wife," in *The Life Stories of Undistinguished Americans as Told by Themselves*, ed. Hamilton Holt (New York: James Pott, 1906), 163.

Chapter 5

1. "Woman Is Appointed Live Stock Inspector," *Copper Era* (Clifton, AZ), July 9, 1915.

2. James H. McClintock, *Arizona: Prehistoric, Aboriginal, Pioneer, Modern* (Chicago: S. J. Clarke, 1916), 337.

3. "Woman Is Appointed."

4. "Arizona Woman Is Live Stock Inspector," *Coconino Sun* (Flagstaff, AZ), August 15, 1919.

5. "Doesn't Look Like Bad Man," *Arizona Republic*, February 13, 1912.

6. "W. W. Burner [*sic*] Is Dismissed," *Arizona Republic*, November 13, 1917.

7. "W. W. Burner [*sic*] Is Dismissed."

8. "Arizona Woman Is Live Stock Inspector."

Chapter 6
1. "Many Are Indicted for Conspiracy in Land Frauds," *Arkansas* (Little Rock) *Gazette*, January 22, 1905.

2. Lincoln Steffens, "The Taming of the West," *American Magazine* (1907): 585.

3. "Mitchell and Hermann," *Weekly Gazette-Times* (Corvallis, OR), December 28, 1904.

4. "Accused Man Loves [*sic*] in Home of Luxury," *San Francisco Examiner*, May 16, 1904.

5. "S. A. D. Puter to Write Book," *Berkeley* (California) *Gazette*, September 17, 1906.

6. "Accused Man."

7. *United States v Mitchell*, 141 F. 666 (1905), cite.case.law/f/141/666/.

8. Jerry A. O'Callaghan, "Senator Mitchell and the Oregon Land Frauds, 1905," *Pacific Historical Review* 21, no. 3 (August 1952): 255.

9. John Messing, "Public Lands, Politics, and Progressives: Oregon Land Fraud Trials, 1903–1910," *Pacific Historical Review* 35, no. 1 (February 1966): 49, wrote that the prosecutor tried to establish that "Puter and Mrs. Watson had lived together as man and wife and had traveled together under various assumed names in order to show that they had conspired together to defraud the government."

10. Steffens, "Taming of the West," 600.

11. Steffens, "Taming of the West," 594.

12. Steffens, "Taming of the West," 592.

13. Steffens, "Taming of the West," 592.

14. "Very Smooth Woman," *Sterling* (Illinois) *Standard*, April 5, 1904.

15. S. A. D. Puter, *Looters of the Public Domain* (Portland, OR: Portland Printing House, 1908), 118.

16. "Very Smooth Woman."

17. Puter, *Looters of the Public Domain*, 114.

18. Puter, *Looters of the Public Domain*, 118.

19. Puter, *Looters of the Public Domain*, 119.

20. "Going to Portland, Ore., under a Heavy Guard," *Tennessean* (Nashville), April 5, 1904.

21. "Accused Woman Is Calmly Indifferent," *San Francisco Examiner*, May 3, 1904.

22. Puter, *Looters of the Public Domain*, 216. See also Steven L. Piott, *Audacious Scoundrels: Stories of the Wicked West* (Guilford, CT: TwoDot, 2021), 177.

23. Puter, *Looters of the Public Domain*, 254.

24. "To Go Scot Free," *Morning Oregonian* (Portland), September 18, 1906.

25. "Mrs. Watson Leaves Jail," *Athena Press* (OR), September 21, 1906.

Chapter 7

1. "Life History of Emma Bell," *Great Falls* (MT) *Tribune*, July 2, 1902; "Unbranded Stock Are Her Undoing," *Butte* (MT) *Inter Mountain*, August 4, 1902.

2. "Realized Money on the Calves," *Butte* (MT) *Miner*, July 30, 1902.

3. "Unbranded Stock."

4. "Unbranded Stock."

5. "State's Penal Colony," *Billings* (MT) *Weekly Gazette*, January 8, 1904.

6. "Helping Hand to Emma Bell," *Independent-Record* (Helena, MT), February 10, 1904.

7. "Application for Pardon," *River Press* (Fort Benton, MT), February 24, 1904.

Part IV

1. "The Life Story of a Farmer's Wife," in *The Life Stories of Undistinguished Americans as Told by Themselves*, ed. Hamilton Holt (New York: James Pott, 1906), 153–54.

2. "Life Story of a Farmer's Wife," 158.

Chapter 8

1. "Memphis Female College," *Memphis* (TN) *Daily Appeal*, June 21, 1873.

2. "She's Winning Her Way," *Great Falls* (MT) *Tribune*, May 22, 1891.

3. "She's Winning Her Way."

4. "Olives," *Sacramento* (CA) *Bee*, December 14, 1889.

5. "Orchard and Farm," *Daily Alta California* (San Francisco), March 23, 1890.

6. "Northern Citrus Fair," *Sacramento* (CA) *Daily Record-Union*, January 14, 1891.

7. "Northern Citrus Fair."

8. "Future Citrus Fairs," *Sacramento* (CA) *Daily Record-Union*, January 20, 1892.

9. "She's Winning Her Way."

10. "She's Winning Her Way."

11. "She's Winning Her Way."

12. "Midwinter Fair," *Los Angeles Herald*, January 1, 1894.

13. California Midwinter Exposition, *Official Guide to the California Midwinter Exposition in Golden Gate Park* (San Francisco: G. Spaulding, 1894), 18.

14. "Midwinter Fair Notes," *Placer Herald* (Rocklin, CA), March 24, 1894.

15. "Ten Thousand Youthful Minds Acquire Education by the Socratic Method," *San Francisco Chronicle*, December 2, 1902.

Chapter 9

1. A. B. MacDonald, "Kansas Queen Points out the Glories of Her Domain," *Kansas City Star*, November 25, 1928; "Hail to the Queen," *New York Times*, July 29, 1932.

2. MacDonald, "Kansas Queen."

3. MacDonald, "Kansas Queen."

4. "Kansas' Real Wheat Queen Is Not White Collar Executive; She Gets into Fields," *Hutchinson* (KS) *News*, July 25, 1929.

5. Ken Burns and Dayton Duncan, *The Dust Bowl: An Illustrated History* (San Francisco: Chronicle Books, 2012), 29. See also Division of Continuing Education, University of Kansas, *Making Do and Doing Without: Kansas in the Great Depression* (Lawrence: Division of Continuing Education, KANU, University of Kansas, 1983), 7.

6. MacDonald, "Kansas Queen."

7. MacDonald, "Kansas Queen"; "The Fairy Story of the 'Short Grass Country' That Became a Vast Field of Golden Wheat," *Kansas City Star*, November 4, 1928.

8. MacDonald, "Kansas Queen."

9. MacDonald, "Kansas Queen."

10. For more about the Federal Farm Board, read David E. Hamilton, "Herbert Hoover: Domestic Affairs," University of Virginia Miller Center, n.d., https://miller center.org/president/hoover/domestic-affairs.

11. "Wheat Queen Tells of Southwest Kansas," *Dodge City* (KS) *Journal*, August 29, 1929.

12. "Kansas Farmers to Store Wheat," *Wichita* (KS) *Eagle*, July 3, 1931.

13. *United States Congressional Serial Set* (Washington, DC: US Government Printing Office, 1933), 1.

14. *United States Congressional Serial Set*, 47.

15. *United States Congressional Serial Set*, 48.

16. *United States Congressional Serial Set*, 48.

17. "A Wheat Queen Is Sorely Tried," *Manhattan* (KS) *Mercury*, July 27, 1932; "Hail to the Queen."

18. "Hail to the Queen."

19. MacDonald, "Kansas Queen."

Chapter 10

1. D. F. Harrington, "What a South Dakota Lady Has Accomplished in Horticulture," in *First Annual Report of the South Dakota State Horticultural Society* (Aberdeen, SD: News Printing, 1904), 98.

2. Liz Almlie, "The Queen of Orchardists: Laura Alderman," *History in South Dakota* (blog), March 1, 2016, historysouthdakota.wordpress.com/2016/03/01/the-queen-of-orchardists/.

3. M. E. Hinkley, "Highways and Hedges," *Report of the Iowa State Horticultural Society* 32 (1897): 298.

4. "A Woman Apple Grower," *Sioux City* (IA) *Journal*, January 19, 1901.

5. "The Territorial Horticultural Exhibit," *Dakota Huronite* (Huron, SD), October 1, 1885.

6. "Fair Notes—Finis," *Daily Plainsman* (Huron, SD), September 13, 1886.

7. "A Day at Dakota's Territorial Fair," *Jasper* (IN) *Weekly Courier*, October 14, 1887.

8. "A Fruit Farm," *Argus-Leader* (Sioux Falls, SD), October 22, 1896.

9. "Woman Apple Grower"; "What They Have Done," *Waukegan* (IL) *Weekly Sun*, January 1, 1898.

10. "A Woman's Orchards," in *Friends' Intelligencer and Journal*, vol. 58 (United States: Friends' Intelligencer Association, 1901), 770; "Woman Orchardist," *Buffalo* (NY) *Evening News*, January 3, 1901.

11. "Mrs. Laura Alderman, Who Owns the Largest Apple Orchard in S. Dakota," *Frank Leslie's Weekly*, October 19, 1901.

12. "Woman Orchardist."

13. "Woman Apple Grower."

14. "Woman Apple Grower."

15. "Woman Apple Grower."

16. "Woman Orchardist."

17. Harrington, "What a South Dakota Lady," 99–100.

Part V

1. "The Life Story of a Farmer's Wife," in *The Life Stories of Undistinguished Americans as Told by Themselves*, ed. Hamilton Holt (New York: James Pott, 1906), 154.

Chapter 11

1. Marie Dille, "Women Who Lead the Way," *Yonkers* (NY) *Herald*, October 13, 1915.

2. Ida Smith, "State Woman Depicts Vivid Era in Paint," *Arizona Republic*, September 13, 1953.

3. Smith, "State Woman."

4. Smith, "State Woman."

5. "Elko Rodeo Calls the Wild," *Nevada State Journal*, August 31, 1914.

6. "Rodeo to Be Biggest Ever," *Reno* (NV) *Gazette-Journal*, August 13, 1914.

7. "Elko Rodeo Calls the Wild."

8. Dille, "Women Who Lead."

9. "Second Day Rodeo," *Weekly Independent* (Elko, NV), September 11, 1914.

10. Dille, "Women Who Lead."

11. Harold O. Weight, "Artist of Copper Canyon," *Desert Magazine*, August 1948, 20.

12. Dille, "Women Who Lead."

13. "Large Crowd in Attendance Second 'Stampede' Day," *Salt Lake* (UT) *Herald-Republican*, July 6, 1913.

14. Weight, "Artist of Copper Canyon," 20.

15. Weight, "Artist of Copper Canyon," 20.

16. Smith, "State Woman."

17. Weight, "Artist of Copper Canyon," 20.

18. Smith, "State Woman."

Chapter 12

1. Ollie Osborn, interview by Harriet Baskas, Oregon Historical Society Library, September 1981, tape side 2.

2. Ollie Osborn, tape side 1.

3. "Championships Are Prizes in Today's Round-up Contests," *Oregon Daily Journal* (Portland), September 26, 1914.

4. "New Round-up Thrills Are Promised," *Oregon Sunday Journal* (Portland), September 12, 1915.

5. Ollie Osborn, tape side 1.

6. Ollie Osborn, tape side 1.

7. Ollie Osborn, tape side 1.

8. Ollie Osborn, tape side 2.

9. Ollie Osborn, tape side 2.

10. "Hall of Fame Honors Three," *East Oregonian*, May 15, 2009.

11. Ollie Osborn, tape side 2.

12. Ollie Osborn, tape side 1.

13. Ollie Osborn, tape side 2.

Part VI

1. "The Life Story of a Farmer's Wife," in *The Life Stories of Undistinguished Americans as Told by Themselves*, ed. Hamilton Holt (New York: James Pott, 1906), 162.

Chapter 13

1. "How Two Spokane Girls Won Homes and Health in the Forest," *Spokesman-Review* (Spokane, WA), July 9, 1911.

2. Dee Garceau, "Single Women Homesteaders and the Meaning of Independence: Places on the Map, Places in the Mind," *Frontiers: Journal of Women Studies* 15, no. 3 (1995): 2.

3. "How Two Spokane Girls Won Homes"; Garceau, "Single Women Homesteaders," 2.

4. "How Two Spokane Girls Won Homes."

5. "How Two Spokane Girls Won Homes."

6. "How Two Spokane Girls Won Homes."

7. Garceau, "Single Women Homesteaders," 7.

8. "How Two Spokane Girls Won Homes."

9. "How Two Spokane Girls Won Homes."

10. "How Two Spokane Girls Won Homes."

Chapter 14

1. "Flint Lock's Widow," *Courier-Journal* (Louisville, KY), February 2, 1884, 2.

2. "Flint Lock's Widow."

3. Dydia DeLyser, " 'Thus I Salute the Kentucky Daisey's Claim': Gender, Social Memory, and the Mythic West at a Proposed Oklahoma Monument," *Cultural Geographies* 15, no. 1 (2008): 71, jstor.org/stable/44251194.

4. *The Eclectic Teacher and Southwestern Journal of Education: For Teachers and Friends of Education* (Louisville, KY: Eclectic Teacher, 1880), 89.

5. "The Public Schools," *Courier-Journal* (Louisville, KY), December 23, 1883.

6. "A Dashing Western Woman," *Harrisburg* (PA) *Daily Independent*, May 27, 1892.

7. "Frankfort on the Kentucky," *Owensboro* (KY) *Messenger*, December 13, 1881.

8. "The Land League," *Courier-Journal* (Louisville, KY), August 6, 1883.

9. For more information, see Oklahoma History Center, *The Opening of Oklahoma* (Oklahoma City: Oklahoma Historical Society, n.d.), okhistory.org/pdf/openingofokla homa.pdf.

10. DeLyser, " 'Thus I Salute,' " 67.

11. "Crazy Daisey," *Courier-Journal* (Louisville, KY), May 3, 1892.

12. "Crazy Daisey."

13. "A Woman Killed in the Wild Rush," *Alexandria* (VA) *Gazette*, September 30, 1891.

14. "Crazy Daisey."

15. "Woman Killed."

16. "Annetta Daisy's Amazons," *New York Times*, April 16, 1892. See also DeLyser, " 'Thus I Salute,' " 67.

17. "A Dashing Western Woman," *Harrisburg* (PA) *Daily Independent*, May 27, 1892.

18. "The First Woman in Oklahoma," *Missoulian* (Missoula, MT), November 14, 1903; "Women to Fore in Oklahoma," *Daily Arkansas Gazette* (Little Rock), March 20, 1910.

19. "Women to Fore."

20. Stan Hoig, "Daisey, Nanitta R. H.," in *Encyclopedia of Oklahoma History and Culture* (Oklahoma City: Oklahoma Historical Society, n.d.), okhistory.org/publications/enc/entry.php?entry=DA004.

Chapter 15

1. "Eveville Seeks Man, Only One, as a Cook," *Inter Ocean* (Chicago), April 26, 1908.

2. "Artcraft Institute Guild," in *Directory and Register of Women's Clubs: City of Chicago and Vicinity, 1914; Indorsed by the Board of Ill. Federation of Women's Clubs* (Chicago: Linden Brothers and Harry H. De Clerque, 1917), 43.

3. "Eveville Seeks Man."

4. To learn more about the Carey Act in Idaho, see Hugh T. Lovin, "The Carey Act in Idaho, 1895–1925: An Experiment in Free Enterprise Reclamation," *Pacific Northwest Quarterly* 78, no. 4 (1987): 122–33, jstor.org/stable/40490218.

5. "Girls Turn Farmers," *Sioux City* (IA) *Journal*, August 29, 1909.

6. "Woman Will Run Idaho Farm," *Twin Falls* (ID) *Weekly News*, September 10, 1909.

7. "Superior Soil in Southern Idaho," *Idaho Statesman* (Boise), September 29, 1909.

8. "Girls Turn Farmers."

9. "A Husband or a Farm?" *Chicago Sunday Tribune*, November 7, 1909.

10. "Dry Farmers' Day Exploits New Agricultural Science," *Chicago Examiner*, November 18, 1909.

11. "Wants Dressmakers to Farm," *Chicago Tribune*, April 6, 1910.

12. "Wants Dressmakers to Farm."

Part VII

1. "The Life Story of a Farmer's Wife," in *The Life Stories of Undistinguished Americans as Told by Themselves*, ed. Hamilton Holt (New York: James Pott, 1906), 158.

Chapter 16

1. Belle van Dorn Harbert, "The Farm Women's Building," in *Dry-Farming and Rural Homes: Official Bulletin of the International Dry-Farming Congress* 8, no. 1 (March 1914): 24.

2. Mrs. Belle V. D. Harbert, "Problems of International Congress of Farm Women," in *Official Proceedings of the Annual Session of the Farmers' National Congress of the United States* (N.p.: The Congress, 1915), 116.

3. "The Farm Woman's Moses," *Sunset: The Pacific Monthly*, July 1914, 757.

4. "Colorado Gets President International Farm Women," *Delta* (CO) *Independent*, March 6, 1914.

5. "The International Congress of Farm Women," *Iron County Record* (Cedar City, UT), June 30, 1911.

6. Mary A. Whedon, "Farm Women Meet," *Farmer's Wife*, December 1, 1912, 214.

7. "A Press Auxiliary," *Home Journal* (Canada: Farmer's Advocate of Winnipeg, 1912), 1546.

8. Whedon, "Farm Women Meet," 214.

9. "Europe Honors Woman," *Rocky Ford* (CO) *Enterprise*, October 24, 1913.

10. "Farm Woman's Moses," 755–56.

11. "Farm Woman's Moses," 757.

12. "Farm Woman's Moses," 757.

13. von Dorn Harbert, "Farm Women's Building," 23.

14. "Scope of the Farm Women's Congress," *Daily Arkansas Gazette* (Little Rock), February 15, 1914.

15. Harbert, "Problems of International Congress of Farm Women," 118.

16. Harbert, "Problems of International Congress of Farm Women," 116.

17. Cherisse Jones-Branch, "An Uneasy Alliance: Farm Women and the United States Department of Agriculture, 1913–1965," *Federal History*, no. 10 (April 2018): 101.

18. Harbert, "Problems of International Congress of Farm Women," 117.

19. Harbert, "Problems of International Congress of Farm Women," 116.

20. Harbert, "Problems of International Congress of Farm Women," 121.

21. "The Smith-Lever Act of 1914," National Archives Foundation, n.d., archivesfoundation.org/documents/smith-lever-act-1914/.

22. van Dorn Harbert, "Farm Women's Building," 24.

23. "Farm Women Will Hold One Session," *Bee* (Omaha, NE), September 30, 1915.

Chapter 17
1. "Montana Stock," *Bismarck* (ND) *Tribune*, October 27, 1882.
2. "Bazoo Gossip," *Sedalia* (MO) *Weekly Bazoo*, June 21, 1892.
3. Ishbel Ross, *Ladies of the Press* (New York: Harper and Brothers, 1936), 146.
4. Pamela J. Creedon, ed., *Women, Media, and Sport: Challenging Gender Values* (Thousand Oaks, CA: Sage, 1994), 69.
5. Ross, *Ladies of the Press*, 145.
6. "A Lady Stock Reporter," *Indiana State Sentinel* (Indianapolis), October 20, 1874.
7. "A Female Cattle Market Reporter," *Republican* (Woodville, MS), February 19, 1870.
8. Ross, *Ladies of the Press*, 145.
9. Ross, *Ladies of the Press*, 148.
10. "Lady Stock Reporter."
11. "Woman's World in Paragraphs," *St. Joseph* (MO) *Weekly Herald*, June 30, 1892.
12. Midy Morgan, "Promising Growth of Mane and Tail," *Mower County* (MN) *Transcript*, August 15, 1872.
13. "Management of Vicious Horses," *Buchanan County Bulletin* (Independence, IA), June 27, 1873.
14. Midy Morgan, "Hints to Horseback Riders," *Century Magazine*, November 1881, 146.
15. "Live-Stock," *Chicago Daily Tribune*, March 27, 1879.
16. "The Montana Ranges," *Omaha* (NE) *Daily Bee*, December 6, 1882.
17. "Montana Stock."
18. Midy Morgan, "The American Beef Supply," *American Agriculturist* 49, no. 2 (February 1890): 64.
19. "Woman's World in Paragraphs."
20. "Obituary: Miss Midy Morgan," *New York Times*, June 2, 1892.

Chapter 18
1. "The Gospel of the Grape," *Weekly Mercury* (Oroville, CA), August 17, 1888.
2. *Philadelphia Inquirer*, August 13, 1888.
3. "Miss Kate Field's Mission," *Sun* (New York City), December 29, 1888.
4. "Wine Men Want High License," *Voice* (New York City), December 6, 1888.
5. "She Will Assist," *St. Helena* (CA) *Star*, August 17, 1888.
6. W. J. McGee and Martin F. Morris, "In Memoriam: Kate Field, 1840–1896," *Records of the Columbia Historical Society, Washington, DC* 1 (1897): 173, http://www.jstor.org/stable/40066706.
7. Autumn Stanley, "Scribbling Women as Entrepreneurs: Kate Field (1838–96) and Charlotte Smith (1840–1917)," *Business and Economic History* 21 (1992): 76.
8. Display ad, *Boston Globe*, November 20, 1884.
9. "Personal and Literary," *Tulare* (CA) *Advance-Register*, September 19, 1888.

10. "An Interviewer's Life," *St. Louis* (MO) *Post-Dispatch*, October 28, 1888.

11. "Dakota Women Endorse Senator Blair and Condemn Kate Field," *Saint Paul* (MN) *Globe*, September 11, 1888.

12. "Kate Field," *San Francisco Chronicle*, March 31, 1889.

13. Annie Nelles Dumond, *The Hard Times: The Cause and the Remedy* (St. Louis, MO: author, 1895), 200.

14. "Kate Field on Prohibition," *Rutland* (VT) *Weekly Herald*, May 2, 1889.

15. "Wines in Washington," *Boston Globe*, December 23, 1888.

16. "Kate Field," *San Francisco Chronicle*.

17. *Times-Democrat* (New Orleans, LA), December 28, 1888.

18. "Kate, the Versatile St. Louisan," *St. Louis* (MO) *Globe-Democrat*, July 30, 1882.

19. "A Feminine Bohemian," *Rutland* (VT) *Daily Herald*, May 13, 1878.

20. "Kate, the Versatile St. Louisan"; "Feminine Bohemian."

21. McGee and Morris, "In Memoriam," 175.

22. "Organization and Proceedings for 1894–'95 of the Columbia Historical Society," *Records of the Columbia Historical Society, Washington, DC* 1 (1897): 2, https://www.jstor.org/stable/40066699?seq=2#metadata_info_tab_contents; McGee and Morris, "In Memoriam," 175.

Part VIII

1. "The Life Story of a Farmer's Wife," in *The Life Stories of Undistinguished Americans as Told by Themselves*, ed. Hamilton Holt (New York: James Pott, 1906), 162.

Chapter 19

1. Nona Marquis Snyder, "The Lure of the Frozen Trail," *Forest and Stream*, December 1923, 717.

2. Log Book USS *Bear*, May 3, 1890 to November 30, 1890, image 67, catalog.archives.gov/id/6919210.

3. Log Book USS *Bear*, image 62.

4. Log Book USS *Bear*, image 59.

5. "CGC Healy History," United States Coast Guard, US Department of Homeland Security, n.d., pacificarea.uscg.mil/Our-Organization/Area-Cutters/CGC-Healy/History/.

6. Log Book USS *Bear*, image 11.

7. Log Book USS *Bear*, image 70.

8. Dorothy Jean Ray, "Sinrock Mary: From Eskimo Wife to Reindeer Queen," *Pacific Northwest Quarterly* 75, no. 3 (1984): 101, jstor.org/stable/23006506.

9. Ray, "Sinrock Mary," 103.

10. Ray, "Sinrock Mary," 105.

11. Ray, "Sinrock Mary," 107.

Chapter 20

1. "Mrs. Pearson an Extensive Breeder of Ostriches," *Omaha* (NE) *Daily Bee*, May 26, 1907.
2. "Ostrich Farming," *Californian* (Salinas), March 30, 1900.
3. "An Arizona Ostrich Farm," *Poughkeepsie* (NY) *Daily Eagle*, January 29, 1902.
4. "Mrs. Pearson an Extensive Breeder."
5. "Mrs. Pearson an Extensive Breeder."
6. "Facts about Ostrich Farms," *Democrat and Chronicle* (Rochester, NY), July 31, 1904.
7. "Mrs. Pearson an Extensive Breeder."
8. "Mrs. Pearson an Extensive Breeder."
9. "Facts about Ostrich Farms."
10. "Mrs. Pearson an Extensive Breeder."
11. "Mrs. Pearson an Extensive Breeder."
12. "Mrs. Pearson an Extensive Breeder."
13. "Mrs. Pearson an Extensive Breeder."
14. "Mrs. Pearson an Extensive Breeder."
15. "Mrs. Pearson an Extensive Breeder."

Chapter 21

1. "Last Texas Buffalo May Be Exterminated," *Brownsville* (TX) *Herald*, August 4, 1931.
2. E. J. Davison, "The Buffaloes of Goodnight Ranch," *Ladies' Home Journal*, February 1901, 7.
3. Glenda Riley, *Women and Nature: Saving the "Wild" West* (Lincoln: University of Nebraska Press, 1999), 113.
4. William T. Hagan, *Charles Goodnight: Father of the Texas Panhandle* (Norman: University of Oklahoma Press, 2007), 21.
5. Hagan, *Charles Goodnight*, 8.
6. Phebe K. Warner, "Pioneers Establish Their Home in Texas' Most Beautiful Spot," *El Paso* (TX) *Herald*, May 30, 1925.
7. "Palo Duro Canyon State Park," Texas Parks and Wildlife, n.d., tpwd.texas.gov/state-parks/palo-duro-canyon/park_history.
8. Olive King Dixon, "Col. Charles Goodnight's Own Story of How He First Entered Palo Duro Canyon to Make a Permanent Home," *Fort Worth* (TX) *Star-Telegram*, February 16, 1936; "Last Texas Buffalo."
9. Dixon, "Col. Charles Goodnight's Own Story."
10. Warner, "Pioneers Establish Their Home."
11. Hagan, *Charles Goodnight*, 49.
12. For more about the effect of the destruction of the bison on Indigenous communities, see J. Weston Phippen, "Kill Every Buffalo You Can! Every Buffalo Dead Is an Indian Gone," *Atlantic*, May 13, 2016; and "William T. Hornady on the Extermination of the American Bison," *Annual Report of the Board of Regents of the Smithsonian Institution* (Washington, DC: US Government

Printing Office, 1889), americanyawp.com/reader/17-conquering-the-west/william-t-hornady-on-the-extermination-of-the-american-bison-1889/.

13. Phebe K. Warner, "A Lesson in Conservation," *Fort Worth* (TX) *Star-Telegram*, February 22, 1919.

14. "Buffalo Remnant Saved by Woman," *El Paso* (TX) *Times*, December 20, 1913.

15. Max Bentley, "Colonel Goodnight and Brave Wife, Pioneers of Plains, Recall Early Trials and Tribulations in Western Texas," *Fort Worth* (TX) *Star-Telegram*, March 25, 1924.

16. Davison, "Buffaloes of Goodnight Ranch," 7.

17. "Buffalo Remnant."

18. "Stock Yards Midway," *Kansas City* (MO) *Journal*, September 25, 1899.

19. Bentley, "Colonel Goodnight."

20. Warner, "Lesson."

21. "Last Texas Buffalo."

Chapter 22

1. "Feeding of Cows," *Fresco* (CA) *Morning Republican*, March 15, 1899.

2. Amy Crow Lawrence, "Minnie Eshleman Sherman: Agricultural Pioneer, Social Activist, City Mother" (master's thesis, California State University, August 2004), 51.

3. "Woman Rancher," *Idaho Statesman* (Boise), September 29, 1901.

4. Lawrence, "Minnie Eshleman Sherman," 18, 20–22.

5. Bertha H. Smith, "A Daughter of the Vine," *Sunset: The Pacific Monthly*, January 1913, 95.

6. Smith, "Daughter of the Vine," 95.

7. Smith, "Daughter of the Vine," 95.

8. M. Eshleman Sherman, "Supplementing Alfalfa as Cow Feed," *California Cultivator*, November 2, 1900, 277.

9. "Feeding of Cows."

10. "Feeding of Cows."

11. Lawrence, "Minnie Eshleman Sherman," 33.

12. "Local and Personal Mention," *Booth's Bazoo* (Needles, CA), September 28, 1889.

13. "Rabbit Shows: Dr. Sherman of the Minnewawa Visits Several," *Fresno* (CA) *Morning Republican*, December 20, 1899.

14. "Thousands Throng the Ferry Nave and Marvel at Products of Northern and Central Counties," *San Francisco Chronicle*, December 3, 1902.

15. Lawrence, "Minnie Eshleman Sherman," 68.

16. Lawrence, "Minnie Eshleman Sherman," 93.

17. Lawrence, "Minnie Eshleman Sherman," 115.

18. Smith, "Daughter of the Vine," 98.

19. Smith, "Daughter of the Vine," 96.

Chapter 23

1. "An Open Letter," *Daily Sentinel* (Grand Junction, CO), July 31, 1902.

2. "Honest Man Not Found," *Boston Globe*, February 18, 1902.

3. "Woman Head of a Goat Ranch," *Sacramento* (CA) *Bee*, January 18, 1902.

4. Hon. J. Warner Mills, "The Economic Struggle in Colorado," *Arena*, August 1905, 122.

5. *Daily Sentinel* (Grand Junction, CO), May 13, 1902.

6. "Goats This Time," *Daily Sentinel* (Grand Junction, CO), July 28, 1902.

7. "Goats This Time."

8. "Herd of Goats Slain," *Inter-Mountain Farmer and Ranchman* (Salt Lake City, UT), July 29, 1902.

9. "An Open Letter."

10. "Goats This Time."

11. "Did Not Care," *Akron* (OH) *Daily Democrat*, November 1, 1902.

12. Mills, "Economic Struggle," 123.

13. Mills, "Economic Struggle," 123.

14. "Fought Woman and Goats," *News-Journal* (Mansfield, OH), October 4, 1902.

15. "Made Her Move Her Ranch," *Kansas City* (MO) *Times*, November 4, 1902.

16. "Age and Youth," *Daily Sentinel* (Grand Junction, CO), August 23, 1904.

Part IX

1. "The Life Story of a Farmer's Wife," in *The Life Stories of Undistinguished Americans as Told by Themselves*, ed. Hamilton Holt (New York: James Pott, 1906), 155.

Chapter 24

1. "Montana's Cattle Queen," *Ottawa* (KS) *Weekly Republic*, December 12, 1895.

2. Elizabeth Smith Collins and Charles Wallace, *The Cattle Queen of Montana* (St. James, MN: C. W. Foote, 1894), 55.

3. Smith Collins and Wallace, *Cattle Queen*, 130–31.

4. Smith Collins and Wallace, *Cattle Queen*, 229.

5. "A Cattle Queen," *Brooklyn* (NY) *Citizen*, November 11, 1894.

6. "Great Cattle Queen," *Lead* (SD) *Daily Call*, April 20, 1899.

7. Elizabeth M. Collins, *The Cattle Queen of Montana*, ed. Charles Wallace and Alvin E. Dyer (Spokane, WA: Press of the Dyer Printing, 1914), 247.

8. Collins, *Cattle Queen*, 249.

9. Collins, *Cattle Queen*, 250.

10. Libby acquired the title "aunty" as a result of her work as a nurse. Collins, *Cattle Queen*, 251.

11. Collins, *Cattle Queen*, 252.

12. *Norcatur* (KS) *Register*, October 25, 1895.

13. "A Woman as a Mine Boss," *Philadelphia Inquirer*, May 30, 1897.

14. Collins, *Cattle Queen*, 258.

15. Collins, *Cattle Queen*, 259.

16. David Rose in his article "Good Mob, Bad Mob: Violence and Community in *The Cattle Queen of Montana* (1894)," *Current Objectives of Postgraduate Study* 13 (2012)

discusses Libby's depictions of violence enacted by Indians and White settlers during the westward movement.

17. Collins, *Cattle Queen*, 241.

18. Collins, *Cattle Queen*, 247.

19. Collins, *Cattle Queen*, 207.

Chapter 25

1. "The First of Her Kind," *Kansas City* (MO) *Star*, August 22, 1895.

2. O. James Hazlett, "Cattle Marketing in the American Southwest," *Kansas History* (Summer 1995): 109, Kshs.org/p/kansas-history-summer-1995/15248.

3. "'The American Girl' in the Cattle Commission Business," *Our Mountain Home*, October 9, 1895.

4. "The First of Her Kind," *Kansas City* (MO) *Star*, August 22, 1895.

5. "Cooper versus Monopoly," *Kansas City* (MO) *Star*, March 22, 1894.

6. O. James Hazlett, "Regulation in the Livestock Trade: The Origins and Operations of the Kansas City Livestock Exchange 1886–1921" (thesis, Kansas State University, May 1987), 120–24.

7. "Miss Goodwin Gives Up," *Kansas City* (KS) *Gazette*, January 15, 1896.

8. Hazlett, "Regulation in the Livestock Trade," 43–44.

9. "First of Her Kind."

10. *Indian Chieftain* (Vinita, Indian Territory, OK), August 29, 1895.

11. "'American Girl.'"

12. "First of Her Kind."

13. Hazlett, "Cattle Marketing," 106.

14. "First of Her Kind."

15. *Smith County Journal* (Smith Center, KS), November 14, 1895.

16. "Kansas City Stock Yard Notes," *Advocate*, November 27, 1895.

17. "First of Her Kind."

18. "'American Girl.'"

19. Minutes of the exchange January 25, 1886–June 5, 1899, vol. 3, Kansas City Live Stock Exchange Records (K0158), the State Historical Society of Missouri Research Center, Kansas City, 257.

20. Minutes of the exchange, 265.

21. Minutes of the exchange, 268.

22. "Miss Goodwin Out of Business," *Kansas City* (MO) *Star*, January 18, 1896.

23. "Suit to Dissolve the K. C. Live Stock Exchange," *Garnett* (KS) *Journal*, June 4, 1897; Albert H. Walker, *History of the Sherman Law* (Westport, CT: Greenwood Press, 2000), 133.

24. "Suit to Dissolve."

25. "Miss Jennie M. Goodwin," *Live Stock Inspector* (Woodward, OK), April 1, 1899.

Conclusion

1. Capt. Jack Crawford, "The Lost Creek Literary Club," *Home and Country* (August 1895), 43.

Selected Bibliography

Auburn Webb, Hertha. "D. W. '80 John' Wallace—Black Cattleman, 1875–1939." Master's thesis, Prairie View Agricultural and Mechanical College, August 1957.

Baumler, Ellen. "Justice as an Afterthought: Women and the Montana Prison System." *Montana: The Magazine of Western History*, Summer 2008. montanawomenshistory .org/wp-content/uploads/2017/06/JusticeAsAnAfterthought.pdf.

Bock, Carl E., and Jane H. Bock. "Shrub Densities in Relation to Fire, Livestock Grazing, and Precipitation in an Arizona Desert Grassland." *Southwestern Naturalist* 42, no. 2 (June 1997): 188–93.

Brunelle, A., T. A. Minckley, J. Delgadillo, and S. Blissett. "A Long-Term Perspective on Woody Plant Encroachment in the Desert Southwest, New Mexico, USA." *Journal of Vegetation Science* 25, no. 3 (May 2014): 829–38.

Davison, E. J. "The Buffaloes of Goodnight Ranch." *Ladies' Home Journal*, February 1901.

DeLyser, Dydia. " 'Thus I Salute the Kentucky Daisey's Claim': Gender, Social Memory, and the Mythic West at a Proposed Oklahoma Monument." *Cultural Geographies* 15, no. 1 (2008). http://www.jstor.org/stable/44251194.

"The Dust Bowl." National Drought Mitigation Center, University of Nebraska. N.d. drought.unl.edu/dustbowl/Home.aspx.

Edwards, Richard. "Changing Perceptions of Homesteading as a Policy of Public Domain Disposal." *Great Plains Quarterly* 29, no. 3 (Summer 2009): 179–202.

Ehrstine, Glenn, and Lucas Gibbs. "Iowa's Prohibition Plague: Joseph Eiboeck's Account of the Battle over Prohibition, 1846–1900." *Annals of Iowa* 78 (Winter 2019): 1–74.

"Farm Foreclosures." *Encyclopedia of the Great Depression*. Encyclopedia.com. August 22, 2022. encyclopedia.com/economics/encyclopedias-almanacs-transcripts-and-maps/farm-foreclosures/.

Garceau, Dee. "Single Women Homesteaders and the Meaning of Independence: Places on the Map, Places in the Mind." *Frontiers: Journal of Women Studies* 15, no. 3 (1995).

Glasrud, Bruce A., and Michael N. Searles, eds. *Black Cowboys in the American West: On the Range, on the Stage, behind the Badge*. Norman: University of Oklahoma Press, 2016.

Holt, Hamilton, ed. *The Life Stories of Undistinguished Americans as Told by Themselves*. New York: James Pott, 1906.

Lawrence, Amy Crow. "Minnie Eshleman Sherman: Agricultural Pioneer, Social Activist, City Mother." Master's thesis, California State University, August 2004.

Lopp Smith, Kathleen, and Verbeck Smith, eds. *Ice Window: Letters from a Bering Strait Village 1892–1902*. Fairbanks: University of Alaska Press, 2001.

Love, Clara M. "History of the Cattle Industry in the Southwest." *Southwestern Historical Quarterly* 19, no. 4 (April 1916): 370–99.

Marquis Snyder, Nona. "The Lure of the Frozen Trail." *Forest and Stream*, December 1923.

National Cowgirl Museum and Hall of Fame. 2017. cowgirl.net/.

Osborn, Ollie. Interview by Harriet Baskas. Oregon Historical Society Library. September 1981. staff.digitalcollections.ohs.org/informationobject/browse?topLod=0&query=ollie+osborn.

Piott, Steven L. *Audacious Scoundrels: Stories of the Wicked West.* Guilford, CT: TwoDot, 2021.

Pruitt-Young, Sharon. "Slavery Didn't End on Juneteenth: What You Should Know about This Important Day." NPR. June 17, 2021. Npr.org/2021/06/17/1007315228/juneteenth-what-is-origin-observation.

Puter, Stephen A. Douglas. *Looters of the Public Domain.* Portland, OR: Portland Printing House, 1908.

Ray, Dorothy Jean. "Sinrock Mary: From Eskimo Wife to Reindeer Queen." *Pacific Northwest Quarterly* 75, no. 3 (1984): 98–107. jstor.org/stable/23006506.

Reagan, John H. "Reconstruction in Texas." Digital History. 1865. https://www.digital history.uh.edu/disp_textbook.cfm?smtid=3&psid=3680.

Riley, Glenda. *Women and Nature: Saving the "Wild" West.* Lincoln: University of Nebraska Press, 1999.

Rose, David. "Good Mob, Bad Mob: Violence and Community in *The Cattle Queen of Montana* (1894)." *Current Objectives of Postgraduate American Studies* 13 (2012). copas.uni-regensburg.de/article/view/150/180.

Ross, Ishbel. *Ladies of the Press.* New York: Harper and Brothers, 1936.

Scofield, Rebecca. *Outriders: Rodeo at the Fringes of the American West.* Seattle: University of Washington Press, 2019.

Seagraves, Anne. *Roses of the West.* Hayden, ID: Wesanne, 2002.

Sigerman, Harriet. *Land of Many Hands: Women in the American West.* New York: Oxford University Press, 1997.

"Sinrock Mary, the Reindeer Queen." National Park Service. October 26, 2021. nps.gov/people/sinrock-mary-the-reindeer-queen.htm.

Smith Collins, Elizabeth, and Charles Wallace. *The Cattle Queen of Montana.* St. James, MN: C. W. Foote, 1894.

Stanley, Autumn. "Scribbling Women as Entrepreneurs: Kate Field (1838–96) and Charlotte Smith (1840–1917)." *Business and Economic History* 21 (1992). web.archive.org/web/20110606051054/http://coursesa.matrix.msu.edu/~business/bhcweb/publications/BEHprint/v021/p0074-p0083.pdf.

Steffens, Lincoln. "The Taming of the West." *American Magazine,* 1907.

Wade, W. F. "The Girl-Ranchers of California." *Cosmopolitan,* April 1900.

Wallace Branch, Hettye. *The Story of 80 John: A Biography of One of the Most Respected Negro Ranchmen in the Old West.* New York: Greenwich Book, 1960.

Weight, H. O. "Artist of Copper Canyon." *Desert,* August 1948.

Whites, LeeAnn, Mary C. Neth, and Gary R. Kremer, eds. *Women in Missouri History: In Search of Power and Influence.* Columbia: University of Missouri Press, 2004.

About the Author

Cheryl Mullenbach is a former history teacher, newspaper editor, and public television project manager. She is the author of five nonfiction books for young people. The American Library Association named *Double Victory* to its "Amelia Bloomer Top Ten List" in 2014. The FDR Presidential Library and Museum honored her as one of ten authors at their Roosevelt Reading Festival in 2013. *Great Depression for Kids*, *Industrial Revolution for Kids*, *Women in Blue*, and *Torpedoed!* have been included in the National Council for the Social Studies "Notable Trade Books for Young People." The International Literacy Association recognized *Industrial Revolution for Kids* in 2015. Her first title for adult audiences, *Stagecoach Women: Brave and Daring Women of the Wild West*, was published in 2020, and *Women of the Spanish-American War* was released in 2022. She lives in Panora, Iowa.